See the
Wider picture

Spice shop, Karnataka, India

The colourful piles of powder at the front of the shop are not spices but paint or dye. This is used to dye fabrics for saris, the beautiful costumes worn by Indian women.

Do you know what the powders are made of?

CONTENTS

0

Family members; possessives; *have got*

Welcome to Harlow Mill

VOCABULARY
Family members | Months and dates |
Free time activities | Giving opinions |
Sports | Possessions | School subjects |
Skills and abilities

GRAMMAR
Possessive adjectives | Possessive *'s* |
Have got for possession |
There is/are with *some/any* | Articles |
Can | Question words

Vocabulary   Family members

1 Complete the words from the descriptions.

1   Your father's sister is your: **a**unt
2   Your father's sister's child is your: **c** _ _ _ _ _ _
3   Your father's father is your: **g** _ _ _ _ _ _ _
4   Your father's brother is your: **u** _ _ _ _
5   Your mother and father are your: **p** _ _ _ _ _ _
6   Your brother is your father's: **s** _ _

Grammar A   Possessive adjectives

2 Complete the sentences with the correct possessive adjectives.

1   Hi I'm Dave and this is *my* brother. _____ name is Jim.
2   Hi! My name is Petra and this is _____ cousin. _____ name is Anna.
3   Penny and I are sisters. _____ surname is Brown.
4   My parents have got a car. _____ car is blue.
5   Hi! Is _____ name Mark?

Grammar B   Possessive *'s*

3 Choose the correct option.

1   The (*boy's*)/ *boys* name is Gary.
2   My *cousin's / cousins* are Tina and Tom.
3   My *parents / parents'* dog is Rusty.
4   Pam is the *children's / childrens'* mum.
5   *Harry and Jan's / Harry's and Jan's* house is in London.
6   *Kai's brother's / Kais brothers* bike is red.
7   My *aunts / aunts'* names are Vera and Chloe.

Grammar C   *Have got* for possession

4 Make questions and sentences with *have got*.

1   I / two pets; I / a cat and a guinea pig
    I've got two pets. I've got a cat and a guinea pig.
2   A: your cousin / a car / ?   B: No / he / not

    _____

3   we / not / a big house

    _____

4   A: you / a sister / ?   B: yes / I

    _____

5   our teacher / a dog; he / short legs

    _____

6   Linda and Brian / not / a cousin

    _____

1 Write the dates in words.

1   11/02   *the eleventh of February*
2   15/06

3   26/11

4   02/04

5   04/12

6   13/09

7   21/10

8   30/07

Vocabulary A   Free time activities

2 Match words 1–10 with words and phrases a–j to make Word Friends.

1	e	listening	a	TV
2		playing	b	photos
3		surfing	c	relatives
4		tidying	d	to the cinema
5		watching	e	to music
6		going	f	your bedroom
7		doing	g	a book
8		taking	h	computer games
9		visiting	i	nothing
10		reading	j	the internet

Vocabulary B   Giving opinions

3 Complete the opinion adjectives in the sentences.

1   I think this programme is **b o r i n** g.
2   I think this book is **e __ c __ t __ __ __** .
3   I think this film is **t __ __ __ __ b __ e** .
4   I think this photo is **g __ __ __ t** .
5   I think this game is **__ u __** .
6   I think this magazine is **__ n __ __ r __ __ t __ __ g** .

Vocabulary C   Sports

4 Match sports 1–8 with photos A–H.

1	E	cycling	5		volleyball
2		swimming	6		football
3		tennis	7		running
4		basketball	8		judo

Vocabulary Possessions

1 Find words 1–10 in the word search.

1 computer
2 guitar
3 dictionary
4 bike
5 laptop
6 camera
7 poster
8 watch
9 book
10 game

D	I	C	T	I	O	N	A	R	Y
L	B	O	O	K	G	R	C	E	T
O	J	X	A	V	A	E	A	T	P
X	W	K	T	T	P	T	M	U	M
B	P	A	I	O	K	S	E	P	L
D	T	U	T	G	U	O	R	M	N
N	G	P	A	C	P	P	A	O	S
U	A	M	D	F	H	C	T	C	X
L	E	Q	B	I	K	E	A	T	Z
S	K	H	D	V	R	B	I	R	F

2 Match words 1–8 with photos A–H.

A

B

C

D

E

F

G

H

1 [H] trainers
2 ☐ a pencil case
3 ☐ headphones
4 ☐ a helmet
5 ☐ a rucksack
6 ☐ keys
7 ☐ a sports bag
8 ☐ sunglasses

Grammar A There is/are with some/any

3 Make questions and negative and positive sentences with *there is/there are*.

1 a TV / in your bedroom **?**
   Is there a TV in your bedroom?

2 books / in the kitchen ✗
   _____

3 posters / in the classroom ✓
   _____

4 trainers / in your sports bag **?**
   _____

5 keys / on the table ✓
   _____

6 a game / on the computer ✓
   _____

7 a dictionary / in the classroom ✗
   _____

8 an MP3 player / in your rucksack **?**
   _____

Grammar B Articles

4 Choose the correct option.

1 We have *a* / *the* big house and *a* / *the* long garden.
2 *A* / *The* house is very old.
3 There's *a* / *the* lovely big kitchen.
4 *A* / *The* living room is my favourite room. There's *a* / *the* big TV set in there.
5 There are two bathrooms. *A* / *The* big bathroom is my parents'. *A* / *The* small one is for me and my sister.
6 Near our house there's *a* / *the* small park.
7 In *a* / *the* park there are lots of trees.
8 There's also *an* / *the* interesting museum and *a* / *the* sports centre.

1 Use the picture clues to complete the crossword.

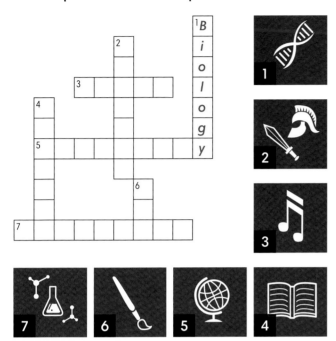

2 Use the pictures and the verbs below to complete sentences 1–8.

| drive play repair speak ~~shoot~~ bake read draw |

1 Dan *can shoot a basketball.*
2 Joe _____
3 Peter _____
4 Chris _____
5 Helen _____
6 Ben _____
7 Jenna _____
8 Beth _____

3 Write questions and short answers for the sentences in Exercise 2.

1 *A: Can Dan shoot a basketball? B: Yes, he can.*
2 _____
3 _____
4 _____
5 _____
6 _____
7 _____
8 _____

4 Choose the correct question words to complete questions 1–6.

| What   How old   Who   Where ~~What time~~   When |

1 A: (your first lesson) *What time is your first lesson?*
   B: At 10.30.
2 A: (your friend / now) _____
   _____
   B: In the cafeteria.
3 A: (your brother) _____
   _____
   B: He's fifteen.
4 A: (your favourite singer) _____
   _____
   B: Sam Smith.
5 A: (your dad's job) _____
   _____
   B: He's a policeman.
6 A: (your next holiday) _____
   _____
   B: In August.

5 Choose the correct option.

1 *Have / (Are)* you sixteen?
2 *Has / Have* you got any brothers?
3 *Are / Is* there a café near your school?
4 *Has / Is* your mum got black hair?
5 *Is / Are* there any posters in your room?
6 *Is / Can* your sister drive a car?
7 *Has / Can* your dad got a Facebook profile?
8 *Are / Can* you learn Italian at your school?

1

Time for culture

I can talk about cultural activities, likes and dislikes.

1 ● Complete the words in the sentences.

1 My friend, Hannah, is an excellent **d**_ancer_.
2 My sister is a great __ **u** __ **i** __ **i** __ __ .
   She can play the piano very well.
3 My favourite **w** __ __ **t** __ __ is J. K. Rowling.
4 My brother's a good **p** __ **o** __ **o** __ __ **a** __ **h** __ __ .
   He's got a cool camera!
5 I don't really like modern art but I quite like old __ **r** __ __ **s** __ **s**
   like Leonardo Da Vinci.
6 I think Benedict Cumberbatch is a very good __ **c** __ __ __ __ .
   He's in lots of great films.

2 ● Find eight words in the word search.

T	I	V	G	I	S	P	A	I	S
K	M	Z	A	X	G	S	A	O	N
U	B	I	N	Q	L	S	R	S	N
E	A	P	I	A	N	O	T	T	H
P	F	Z	S	B	R	K	E	E	D
F	B	Y	N	R	C	L	C	E	L
Z	Z	K	O	O	L	P	H	R	P
E	A	H	R	A	V	T	N	I	D
D	E	A	B	R	R	E	O	E	H
A	A	E	V	V	I	O	L	I	N

3 ● Complete the sentences with the correct words.

| don't   hate   really   into   ~~love~~   interested

1 I *love* flamenco. It's cool!
2 I'm not _____ in graphic novels.
3 I'm _____ acting. I'd love to be an actor.
4 I _____ documentaries. They're so boring!
5 I _____ like dancing much.
6 I'm _____ interested in drawing. I like art.

4 ● WORD FRIENDS Match the parts of the sentences.

1 [d] I like playing   a pictures.
2 [ ] I like listening   b comics.
3 [ ] I like drawing   c photographs.
4 [ ] I like reading   d the violin.
5 [ ] I like watching   e to hip-hop.
6 [ ] I like taking   f cartoons.

5 ●● Complete the words from the descriptions.

1 You can see films in this place: **c**inema
2 This person can paint pictures very well: **a** _ _ _ _ _
3 This is a musical instrument: **v** _ _ _ _ _
4 This is a scary film: **h** _ _ _ _ _
5 This is a funny film: **c** _ _ _ _ _
6 You can do this if you've got a camera: **p** _ _ _ _ _ _ _ _
7 This is a classical type of dancing: **b** _ _ _ _
8 You can read this: **n** _ _ _ _

6 ●● Complete the sentences with the correct words.

| piano salsa director ~~comedy~~ |
| short stories rock |

1 This is my favourite *comedy* . It's really funny.
2 I want to learn to play the _____.
3 I've got a really good book of _____. I read one every day.
4 I know all the actors in the film but not the _____.
5 I want to go to _____ classes. It's a great dance!
6 I love _____ music and I always listen to it in my room.

7 ●● Use the letters to write the correct words.

1 I like TRACIMON *romantic* films but I prefer DEMISOEC _____.
2 I'm really into NICNAGD _____ and I'd like to go to BUZAM _____ classes.
3 Our teacher is a great ISNAUMIC _____ and he can play the RIGTUA _____.
4 People who are good at GRINDAW _____ can make TROCNOA _____ films.
5 I hate DREGANI _____ but I like TWICGHAN _____ films.

8 ●●● Choose the correct option.

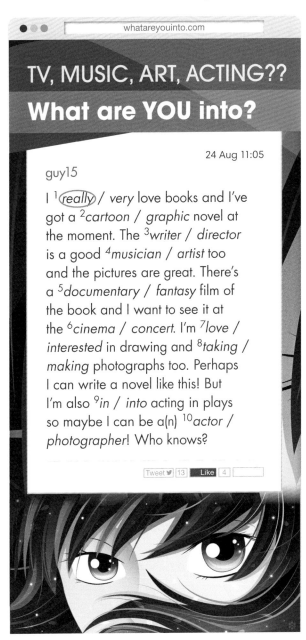

whatareyouinto.com

TV, MUSIC, ART, ACTING??
What are YOU into?

24 Aug 11:05

guy15

I [1](really)/ *very* love books and I've got a [2]*cartoon* / *graphic* novel at the moment. The [3]*writer* / *director* is a good [4]*musician* / *artist* too and the pictures are great. There's a [5]*documentary* / *fantasy* film of the book and I want to see it at the [6]*cinema* / *concert*. I'm [7]*love* / *interested* in drawing and [8]*taking* / *making* photographs too. Perhaps I can write a novel like this! But I'm also [9]*in* / *into* acting in plays so maybe I can be a(n) [10]*actor* / *photographer*! Who knows?

Tweet 🐦 13   Like 4

9 ●●● Complete the blog post with the correct form of the word in brackets.

●●●   terrymac

My interests

I really like [1]*dancing* (dance)! I love [2]_____ (classic) music and I'm not a bad [3]_____ (music). I can play the piano quite well. I don't like [4]_____ (read) books much, but I like short stories because they're quick! And I'm interested in [5]_____ (watch) documentaries on TV – if they're about famous [6]_____ (dance)! I'm also into [7]_____ (photograph) and I like [8]_____ (take) photos of my friends in dance classes.

Tweet 🐦 13   Like 4

I can use the Present Simple to talk about habits and routines.

1 ● **Complete the sentences with the correct affirmative form of the verbs in brackets.**

1 My brother *likes* (like) hip-hop.
2 My friends _____ (go) to a café after school.
3 I _____ (play) computer games.
4 My teacher _____ (write) poems.
5 I _____ (speak) English.
6 My English friend _____ (live) in London.

2 ● **Write the negative forms of the sentences in Exercise 1.**

1 *My brother doesn't like hip-hop.*
2 _____
3 _____
4 _____
5 _____
6 _____

3 ● **Put the adverbs of frequency in brackets in the correct place in the sentences.**

1 We go to the cinema. (never)
We never go to the cinema.
2 I read short stories. (sometimes)
_____
3 My brother is in his room. (always)
_____
4 I'm interested in new songs. (always)
_____
5 My mum goes to Zumba classes on Mondays. (usually)
_____
6 My classmates are bored in Mr Tutt's classes! (never)
_____

4 ●● **Correct the sentences.**

1 I never does my homework before dinner.
I never do my homework before dinner.
2 My sister sometimes like listening to techno.
_____
3 He goes always to bed at 10.30.
_____
4 My favourite actor don't act in horror films.
_____
5 She never is at home before 8.30.
_____
6 We play often games in our English class.
_____

5 ●● **Order the words to make sentences.**

1 like / Hannah / reading / doesn't / much
Hannah doesn't like reading much.
2 computer / with / often / friends / I / my / games / play
_____
3 understand / I / Spanish / don't
_____
4 buy / online / I / clothes / usually
_____
5 teacher / car / drive / doesn't / our / a
_____
6 never / for / Tom / class / late / is
_____

6 ●●● **Complete the text with the correct form of the verbs in brackets.**

I often ¹*go* (go) to the cinema with my friends at the weekend. We ² _____ (not go) in the evenings because we ³ _____ (do) our homework then. Our teacher ⁴ _____ (not be) happy if we ⁵ _____ (give) homework in late!
At the cinema we usually ⁶ _____ (watch) action films because they're exciting. I like romantic films but my best friend ⁷ _____ (not like) them, so sometimes I ⁸ _____ (watch) romantic films on DVD at home. It's good because my sister often ⁹ _____ (watch) them with me. It's always nice to watch a film with someone else!

1.3 | **READING and VOCABULARY** | Do young people watch a lot of TV?

I can find specific detail in an article and talk about age groups.

PEOPLE TODAY WATCH TV IN DIFFERENT WAYS

OUR READERS TELL US ABOUT HOW THEY AND THEIR FAMILIES WATCH TV.

1
e I usually watch TV in my room but sometimes I watch it with my family. That's good because we don't often spend a lot of time together. Also we can talk about the film or programme and sometimes have arguments! But one problem is that my family often disagrees about what they want to watch! So, in my room I can choose my own programmes.

2 Also today we don't need to watch live TV. When I'm out I record my favourite programme and watch it later. That way you can cut all the advertisements – which is great! My best friend watches TV online. She says it's better because she can watch anything at any time! But she gets the adverts!

3 My brother never watches much TV because he spends all his time checking different channels. He watches for a few minutes and then gets bored and looks for another programme! In the end he never watches a complete programme.

4 My dad doesn't have much time to watch TV during the week so he gets DVDs of all his favourite programmes. Then at the weekend he watches about four hours of shows like *Downton Abbey*! They say teenagers get 'square eyes' but in our family it's my dad.

1 Read the text. Match paragraphs 1–4 with headings a–e. There is one extra heading.

a   The right time for you
b   A new way to watch TV
c   Marathon TV
d   Too much choice?
e   With others or alone?

2 Read the text again. Mark the sentences ✓ (right), ✗ (wrong) or ? (doesn't say).

1   ☒   The writer's family does a lot of things together.
2   ☐   They usually have the same opinions.
3   ☐   The writer prefers programmes without breaks.
4   ☐   The writer's brother doesn't like watching TV.
5   ☐   The writer likes *Downton Abbey*.
6   ☐   The writer's father works in the evenings.

3 Complete the sentences with the correct words from the text.

live   online   ~~channel~~   advertisements

1   I want to watch the new documentary tonight. Which _channel_ is it on?
2   I often watch TV _____ because I'm out a lot in the evenings.
3   When I watch a film and the _____ come on, I go out and make a cup of tea or something!
4   My mum and dad never record programmes. They always watch _____ TV.

4 Choose the correct option.

1   My grandparents are *middle aged* / (*pensioners*) and they often watch TV during the day.

2   My brother is a *teenager* / *kid* and watches a lot of children's programmes.

3   *Teenagers* / *Adults* can't watch too much TV when they have exams.

4   There are many programmes about buying houses during the day. A lot of *teenagers* / *pensioners* watch them.

I can ask and answer questions about habits and routines.

1 ● **Write the questions.**

1 Q: Where *does he live*?
   A: He lives in London.

2 Q: When _____?
   A: I start school at 9.30.

3 Q: What _____?
   A: They do homework in the evenings.

4 Q: What _____?
   A: My sister likes reading poems.

5 Q: How often
   _____?
   A: We go to dance classes twice a week.

6 Q: What time
   _____?
   A: The film finishes at 7.30.

2 ● **Make questions from the prompts.**

1 you / like / modern art / ?
  Do you like modern art?

2 your sister / speak French / ?
  _____

3 Mr Jacobs / live in a big house / ?
  _____

4 Jack / play an instrument / ?
  _____

5 your dad / work in the city / ?
  _____

6 your classmates / listen to rap music / ?
  _____

3 ● **Write short answers for the questions in Exercise 2.**

1 Yes, *I do*.
2 No, _____ .
3 Yes, _____ .
4 No, _____ .
5 Yes, _____ .
6 Yes, _____ .

4 ●● **Complete the dialogue with the correct words.**

A: ¹**Do** your parents work?

B: Yes, ²_____ do. They both work.

A: ³_____ your mum work every day?
B: Yes, she ⁴_____ . She's a teacher.
A: ⁵_____ she teach at your school?
B: No, she ⁶_____ . I'd hate that!
A: ⁷_____ does she teach?
B: She teaches at Garfield High School.
A: Which school ⁸_____ you go to?
B: I go to Minchester Academy.
A: ⁹_____ you like it there?
B: Yes, I ¹⁰_____ . It's a great school.
A: ¹¹_____ do you do in your free time?
B: I play football and I listen to music.
A: ¹²_____ often do you play football?
B: About ¹³_____ or twice a week.

5 ●●● **Complete the email with the correct form of the verbs in brackets.**

To: hello@jenna.com

Hi Jenna,

I'm really glad you're my online English friend. Please tell me something about yourself! Where ¹*do you live* (you/live)? ²_____ (you/have) any brothers and sisters? ³_____ (they/go) to school too or ⁴_____ (they/work)? ⁵_____ (you/like) music? What type of music ⁶_____ (you/like)? What magazines ⁷_____ (you/usually read)? ⁸_____ (you/often go) to other countries on holiday? And ⁹_____ (you/speak) MY language? Sorry to ask so many questions. I'm really interested!

Best wishes,

Lucia

6 **Match sentences 1–5 with responses a–e.**   **O**UT of class

1 [d] Do you like the band *Maroon 5*?
2 [ ] Do you want to go for a coffee?
3 [ ] Do you watch *Teen Wolf*?
4 [ ] Where is Gary?
5 [ ] Jim says he speaks ten languages!

a To be honest, I'm not really into it.
b Not right now.
c Yeah, right!
d They're awesome!
e I've no idea.

I can identify specific detail in a conversation and talk about media habits.

1 Match the types of media 1–8 with photos A–H.

1 [B] talk show
2 [ ] horoscope
3 [ ] news headlines
4 [ ] documentary
5 [ ] soap opera
6 [ ] reality show
7 [ ] game show
8 [ ] weather forecast

2 Match comments 1–8 with the types of media from Exercise 1.

1 They say that today is a good day for me!
horoscope
2 I know all the answers. _____
3 That singer is awesome! _____
4 It's really interesting and the photography is beautiful. You can learn a lot. _____
5 That's the man's girlfriend. They're always angry! _____
6 That's my favourite sportsman. They also have my favourite actor and comedian on today. _____
7 Yes, it's sunny all week! _____
8 That's terrible! I hope the people are all right. _____

3 🔊 02 **Read the survey. Then listen and match speakers A–E with questions 1–8. There are three extra questions.**

quickonlinesurvey.com

TAKE OUR QUICK ONLINE SURVEY!

1 Do you think teenagers are interested in current affairs programmes on TV?   A [8]
2 What's your favourite type of documentary?
3 Does anyone in your family watch a lot of sport on TV?   B [ ]
4 How often do you watch soap operas?
5 Why do people like watching talk shows?   C [ ]
6 Do you go to see films because of TV film reviews?
7 Do you want to go on a TV game show?   D [ ]
8 Do you enjoy watching reality TV?   E [ ]

4 🔊 02 **Listen again. Match speakers A–E with comments 1–6. There is one extra comment.**

1 [ ] I think people sometimes have the wrong idea about teenagers.
2 [ ] I like learning about famous people.
3 [A] I enjoy watching people who disagree.
4 [ ] I don't want people to laugh at me.
5 [ ] I argue about talent shows.
6 [ ] I think a programme can help people.

I can buy a ticket at the cinema.

1 Match words 1–5 with words a–e to make Word Friends.

OUT of class

1	e	sold	a	way
2	☐	front	b	on
3	☐	hold	c	row
4	☐	no	d	on
5	☐	come	e	out

2 Complete the sentences with the correct Word Friends from Exercise 1.

OUT of class

1 I'm sorry there aren't any tickets for the film. It's _sold out_.
2 I don't want to pay £20 for a ticket! _____!
3 If you sit in the _____ you can't see the screen very well.
4 _____! Isn't that your ticket?
5 I really want to see that film. _____, please!

3 Match questions 1–4 with answers a–d.

1	c	What's on?
2	☐	Can I have three tickets for *True Blue*?
3	☐	How much is that?
4	☐	Here you are.

a That's £20.
b Thanks. Enjoy the film.
c A fantasy film, *True Blue*.
d Sure, which screening?

4 Complete the dialogue with the correct phrases.

> No way   Here you are   which screening
> I'd like   That's   Enjoy the film   ~~Let's go~~
> What's on   Can I have   Come on

A: ¹**Let's go** to the cinema.
B: OK. ² _____ ?
A: Well, there's *Five Lives*. That's a horror film.
B: ³ _____ ! I don't like horror films.
A: ⁴ _____ .
B: Well, OK. ⁵ _____ two tickets for *Five Lives*, please?
C: Sure, ⁶ _____ ?
B: The 7.30.
C: I'm sorry, it's sold out … Oh, no, hold on! There are two seats in the front row.
B: OK. ⁷ _____ two tickets, please. How much is that?
C: ⁸ _____ £16.80, please.
B: ⁹ _____ .
C: Thank you. ¹⁰ _____ .

5 🔊 03 Complete the dialogues with the correct sentences. Then listen and check.

A

A: ¹**b**
B: The new Jake Larkin film, *Mark of Hell*.
A: ² ___
B: Oh, come on, please!
A: ³ ___
B: In half an hour.

a I don't like action films!
b What's on?
c OK. When does it start?

B

A: I'd like two tickets for *Mark of Hell*, please.
B: ¹ ___
A: The 5.15.
B: ² ___
A: That's fine.
B: ³ ___
A: Here you are.
B: ⁴ ___

a That's fifteen, fifty.
b Sure, which screening?
c Thanks. Enjoy the film.
d There are two seats in row five.

I can write a personal introduction to a webpage.

Ella
Marchwood,
Southampton, England
Romantic ♥

Photo Gallery

● ● ●

Her stories

The red table
Another Monday
Where are you?

Friends

About me

My name is Ella Myers and I'm fifteen. I'm from London and I live in Marchwood. It's a town near Southampton. I have one sister and two brothers and I go to Marchwood High School. I love Art, English and History. I like rock and pop music and my favourite band is *One Republic*. But my passion is books. My favourite books are *The Fault in our Stars* and *Twilight*. In my free time I write short stories. I write one or two pages every day. You can read some of them on my webpage. Tell me if you like them!

Name:	Ella ¹*Myers*
Age:	2 _____
Family:	3 _____
Lives in:	4 _____
From:	5 _____
Nationality:	British
Studies at:	6 _____
Favourite subjects:	7 _____
Music:	8 _____
Favourite band:	9 _____
TV:	dramas, cartoons, reality TV
Films:	romantic, horror, comedies
Books:	10 _____
Likes:	11 _____

1 Read the information about Ella and look at the photos on her webpage. Then read her personal introduction and complete the information.

2 Decide if the sentences give us personal information (P), information about hobbies/interests (H) or information about routines (R).

1 ☐P I have one sister and two brothers.
2 ☐ I go to school by bus every day.
3 ☐ My big passion is books.
4 ☐ My best friend is Patsy.
5 ☐ I live in Marchwood.
6 ☐ I play tennis. I'm really good at it.

3 Complete the sentences with the correct words.

> about   a   favourite   ~~old~~   big   outside
> with   from   hometown

1 I'm fifteen years *old*.
2 I come _____ London.
3 My _____ is Marchwood.
4 I live _____ my family in a small house.
5 I'm mad _____ books.
6 My _____ book is *The Hunger Games*.
7 My _____ passion is writing.
8 _____ school I like tennis and swimming.
9 Once _____ week I go into town with friends.

4 Write a personal introduction for one of your friends.

a Divide the introduction into three paragraphs:
  1 Personal information
  2 Hobbies and interests
  3 Routines
b Make notes for ideas you can put in the paragraphs.
c Write the introduction.

About me

My name is _____

1.8 SELF-ASSESSMENT

For each learning objective, tick (✓) the box that best matches your ability.

☺☺ = I understand and can help a friend.   ☹ = I understand but have some questions.

☺ = I understand and can do it by myself.   ☹☹ = I do not understand.

		☺☺	☺	☹	☹☹	Need help?	Now try ...
1.1	Vocabulary					Students' Book pp. 10–11 Workbook pp. 6–7	Ex. 1–2, p. 15
1.2	Grammar					Students' Book p. 12 Workbook p. 8	Ex. 3–6, p. 15
1.3	Reading					Students' Book p. 13 Workbook p. 9	
1.4	Grammar					Students' Book p. 14 Workbook p. 10	
1.5	Listening					Students' Book p. 15 Workbook p. 11	
1.6	Speaking					Students' Book p. 16 Workbook p. 12	Ex. 7, p. 15
1.7	Writing					Students' Book p. 17 Workbook p. 13	

1.1   I can talk about cultural activities, likes and dislikes.
1.2   I can use the Present Simple to talk about habits and routines.
1.3   I can find specific detail in an article and talk about age groups.
1.4   I can ask and answer questions about habits and routines.
1.5   I can identify specific detail in a conversation and talk about media habits.
1.6   I can buy a ticket at the cinema.
1.7   I can write a personal introduction to a webpage.

What can you remember from this unit?

New words I learned (the words you most want to remember from this unit)	**Expressions and phrases I liked** (any expressions or phrases you think sound nice, useful or funny)	**English I heard or read outside class** (e.g. from websites, books, adverts, films, music)

Vocabulary

1 Complete the words in the sentences.

1 My brother plays the **d** _ _ _ _ _ in a band.
2 I don't enjoy **c** _ _ _ _ _ _ _ _ _ music, like Mozart or Beethoven.
3 My favourite **a** _ _ _ _ _ is James Pattinson.
4 I often watch **r** _ _ _ _ _ _ _ films where people are in love.
5 A lot of children love watching **c** _ _ _ _ _ _ _ _ _, like *Minions* or *How to Train Your Dragon*.
6 My sister wants to go to Cuba to learn **s** _ _ _ _ dancing.

2 Complete the sentences with the correct words.

> drawing   listening   playing
> reading   taking   watching

1 We have a piano but I hate _____ it.
2 My dad is mad about _____ to old music.
3 My mum is really into _____ selfies.
4 I like _____ reviews about new films.
5 Our family loves _____ soap operas together.
6 I don't like _____ pictures in Art at school.

Grammar

3 Order the words to make questions.

1 you / where / live / do / ?
_____

2 work / day / your / every / dad / does / ?
_____

3 do / many / have / lessons / English / a week / you / how / ?
_____

4 do / you / Saturday / swimming / go / every / ?
_____

5 does / how / photos / friend / take / your / often / ?
_____

6 like / sisters / do / your / music / what / ?
_____

4 Match the questions in Exercise 3 with answers a–f.

a ☐ Every day.   d ☐ Hip-hop.
b ☐ Yes, I do.   e ☐ No, he doesn't.
c ☐ Three.   f ☐ In London.

5 Complete the dialogue with *do*, *does*, *don't* or *doesn't*.

A: ¹_____ you like classical music?
B: No, I ²_____ but my sister ³_____.
A: ⁴_____ she like hip-hop music too?
B: No, she ⁵_____ but I ⁶_____!

6 Make sentences or questions from the prompts.

1 I / not / like / documentaries
_____

2 you / want / to go to the cinema / ?
_____

3 my friend / not / live / near me
_____

4 Jack / speak / English and French
_____

5 our teacher / usually / give / us lots of homework
_____

6 what time / you / go to bed on Fridays / ?
_____

Speaking language practice

7 Complete the dialogue with one word in each gap.

A: What's ¹_____ today?
B: There's a horror film and a comedy.
A: ²_____ I have a ticket for the horror film, please?
B: Is that for the 5.00 or the 6.00 ³_____?
A: The five o'clock, please.
B: Sorry, it's ⁴_____ out.
A: OK, for the six o'clock, please.
B: There's a ⁵_____ in the front row.
A: How ⁶_____ is that?
B: That's £10, please.

1 Match dances 1–4 with photos A–D.

1   B   waltz   3   ☐   popping
2   ☐   breaking   4   ☐   swing

2 Complete the sentences with the dances from Exercise 1.

1   *Waltz* and _____ were popular dances a long time ago.

2   _____ and _____ are modern dances.

3 Use the letters to write the correct words.

1   We use the word '**LESTY**' *style* to talk about different ways of dancing.

2   You need to be **BLEFEXIL** _____ to put your arms and legs in different positions.

3   People who are clever at doing something are **FLISKLU** _____.

4   Someone who people like looking at is **TRICATEVAT** _____.

5   A **NIVORSE** _____ is another way of doing the same thing.

6   **STRINOIOMPAIV** _____ is when you invent a dance as you do it.

4 Complete the sentences with the words from Exercise 3.

1   The new singer in the band is very *attractive* with his dark hair and green eyes!

2   Angela is a very _____ dancer and can do the most difficult moves.

3   My friend likes the classical _____ of dancing but I prefer modern dances.

4   There's a new _____ of the ballet *Sleeping Beauty* – they say it's amazing.

5   The dancers are very _____. They can jump and lift their legs over their heads!

6   Sharifa uses _____ to create dances – she thinks of the moves while she's dancing.

5 Complete the adjectives in the sentences.

1   Someone who can write stories and paint pictures is **creat*ive***.

2   Someone who loves something very much is **passion___ ___**.

3   Something that is exciting is **thrill___ ___**.

4   Something that makes you feel free is **liberat___ ___**.

5   Something that you can't stop watching is **hypno___ ___**.

6   Something that makes you feel happy is **uplift___ ___**.

6 Complete the sentences with the adjectives from Exercise 5.

1   A lot of people think dance is *liberating* because they can show their feelings.

2   I wish I was more _____ but I can't sing or paint or dance!

3   This music is _____ and I sometimes go to sleep while listening to it.

4   When I feel sad, I listen to this song because it's _____.

5   My brother is _____ about football and talks about it all the time!

6   There's a _____ moment at the end of the film when two men try to kill the girl.

7 Choose the correct option.

1   Carl is very *hypnotic* / (*flexible*) – he can touch his head with his foot!

2   I don't like the film *style* / *version* of the book.

3   Mark is *passionate* / *thrilling* about rock music and plays it all day.

4   My best friend has blond hair and blue eyes and is very *liberating* / *attractive*.

5   Rap music is *popular* / *skilful* at the moment but I prefer jazz.

8 Read the video script. Underline any words or phrases you don't know and find their meaning in your dictionary.

Young Dancer Competition
Part 1

In this competition there are five dancers in each group and the best ones in each group go through to the grand final. So, let's meet the five dancers in the hip-hop section and learn how and
5   why they dance.

First up is Harry Barnes from Liverpool. Why does he dance? Harry says that dancing is uplifting. If he's feeling sad, he usually puts on a favourite song and just dances. Then he's happy and everything is better. His favourite style is 'popping'. His advice for new
10 dancers? Always, always, always practise – never stop!

Next is Jonadette Carpio. She was born in the Philippines but now she lives in South Wales. Why does she dance? Because dance is very creative. She invents a lot of amazing movements. Her favourite style is 'krumping'. That's a new dance style which is very
15 popular these days. The face is as important as the body. Here, in this dance, she's a prisoner.

Third is Jodelle Douglas. He's from Bristol and he loves 'breaking'. Jodelle dances because dance is his passion. He never stops learning. He meets up with other dancers in Bristol to exchange
20 ideas and learn new steps. They are all passionate about dance. Here he dances in the 'popping' style.

Fourth is Sharifa Tonkmor from London. She loves dance because it's really liberating. Her favourite form of dancing is 'free-styling' or improvisation. She decides her dance style when she dances, not
25 before! She sometimes dances with other people in Charing Cross train station. Sharifa likes dancing to rap music, like this. This type of song makes her really happy.

Last is Kieran Lai from Southend. He loves dance because he thinks it's hypnotic. He dances in the 'popping' style because he
30 loves dancing like a machine. He creates different characters in his dances – heroes and fantasy characters. In this dance, he is the Tin Man from *The Wizard of Oz*. It's thrilling to watch him.

Part 2

So, which of the five dancers is the winner? What do you think?
35 Jonadette, Harry, Sharifa, Kieran or Jodelle? Who do you want to win?

"And the winner of the 2015 BBC Young Dancer Hip-Hop category is Harry Barnes!"

For the judges, he is both a very talented and natural performer.
40 He now goes through to the grand final at a big theatre in London. Watch him again then!

2

Friends and family

I can talk about clothes and appearance.

1 ● Complete the table with the words below.

> ~~belt~~ ~~hoodie~~ ~~striped~~ jacket glasses sweater pyjamas
> tracksuit baggy handbag scarf leather cotton necklace
> trainers cap checked tight

clothes and footwear	accessories	adjectives
hoodie	*belt*	*striped*

2 ● Choose the correct answers.

1 I usually wear __ at the weekends when I go out with my friends.
   a pyjamas   b fancy-dress costume   ⓒ jeans

2 I don't really like wearing __ but I need to wear one for my sister's wedding.
   a tracksuits   b dresses   c underwear

3 My dad works in a bank and he wears a white __ to work.
   a hoodie   b shorts   c shirt

4 I've got a cool __ from the USA with my name on it.
   a piercing   b T-shirt   c jeans

5 It's hot so I need my __ .
   a shorts   b shoes   c boots

6 I wear __ because I can't see very well.
   a glasses   b earrings   c belts

7 My best friend has a __ of a rose on her arm. It's pretty.
   a piercing   b scarf   c tattoo

8 Don't forget your __ . It's cold outside.
   a handbag   b necklace   c scarf

3 ●● Complete the words from the descriptions.

1 You carry things in this when you go out: **h**andbag
2 You wear this round your neck: **n** _ _ _ _ _ _ _
3 You wear this under your clothes: **u** _ _ _ _ _ _ _ _
4 This is a small hole in your body: **p** _ _ _ _ _ _ _
5 You often wear these on your feet: **t** _ _ _ _ _ _ _
6 You wear these in the summer when it's hot: **s** _ _ _ _ _

4 ●● What are the people talking about?

1 They're lovely and warm in bed. *pyjamas*
2 I wear these on my feet when it snows. _____
3 I want to go to the party as a cat! _____
4 I have some in my ears and one in my lip. _____
5 In the summer it keeps my head cool when I do sport. _____
6 My sister puts lots of things in this and carries it everywhere. _____

5 ● WORD FRIENDS Choose the correct answers.

1 Which item can we NOT use with *baggy*?
   a pyjamas   b sweater   ⓒ handbag
2 Which item can we NOT use with *leather*?
   a boots   b glasses   c belt
3 Which item can we NOT use with *woolly*?
   a trainers   b sweater   c hat
4 Which item can we NOT use with *striped*?
   a dress   b pyjamas   c necklace
5 Which item can we NOT use with *tight*?
   a T-shirt   b shoes   c earrings
6 Which item can we NOT use with *checked*?
   a tattoo   b shirt   c jacket
7 Which item does NOT have a *logo*?
   a cap   b piercing   c sweater

6 ●● Match the pairs of sentences.

1 [e] This T-shirt is very baggy.
2 [ ] I wash these jeans a lot.
3 [ ] I like wearing this cotton top.
4 [ ] Can I borrow your woolly hat?
5 [ ] I don't want a striped jacket.
6 [ ] These boots are real leather.

a I prefer a plain one.
b Now they're really tight.
c It's cold outside.
d That's why they're expensive.
e It's because it's my big sister's.
f It's cool in the summer.

7 ●● Answer the clues to complete the crossword.

Across
3 not plain or checked
5 it's pretty and you wear it round your neck
8 it's usually leather and you wear it round your jeans
9 you wear them when you go running
10 a picture or a mark of a company

Down
1 these trousers are usually blue
2 you wear it over a top
4 you can wear it when you train
6 it's a warm top
7 wear it round your neck when it's cold
8 not tight

8 ●●● Complete the words in the text.

Kate's Clothes

Do you want something new to wear at the weekend or for that special party?

Come along to our new shop in the Lake Mall for clothes and ¹a**ccessories**.

We sell everything from casual clothes, like ²__e__s and T-shirts, to dresses and even fancy-dress ³__s__m__ for those special occasions! Do you need sports gear? We sell ⁴__a__e__ for your feet and ⁵r____s____s for your training. All our clothes are modern – if ⁶h__k_d shirts are in fashion you can find them here. Perhaps this year it's ⁷t____e_ jackets? Look for them here! Would you like some ⁸l____h__ boots? We have them. Warm ⁹y____a_ for bedtime? We've got lots. Pretty gold earrings or a silver ¹⁰__c__a___? Right here!

See you soon!

I can talk about present activities.

1 ● Look at the picture and complete the sentences with the Present Continuous form of the correct verbs.

| listen play read check cry lie eat ~~take~~

1 The woman *is taking* a photo.
2 The man _____ a newspaper.
3 The children _____ a computer game.
4 The guard _____ the tickets.
5 The old lady _____ a sandwich.
6 The teenager _____ to music.
7 The dog _____ on the floor.
8 The baby _____.

2 ● Write negative sentences.

1 I'm waiting for Charlie.
   I'm not waiting for Charlie. I'm waiting for Brad.
2 They're studying French.
   _____. They're studying Spanish.
3 She's wearing jeans.
   _____. She's wearing trousers.
4 You're eating a chicken sandwich.
   _____. You're eating a bacon sandwich.
5 We're watching the news.
   _____. We're watching a talk show.
6 He's going to town.
   _____. He's going to work.

3 ● Order the words to make questions.

1 new / wearing / dress / you / a / are / ?
   Are you wearing a new dress?
2 is / shouting / the / teacher / why / ?
   _____
3 the / what / doing / are / boys / ?
   _____
4 are / where / going / you / ?
   _____
5 us / Elise / here / is / meeting / ?
   _____

4 ●● Match questions 1–6 with answers a–f.

1 | *b* | Where are you going?
2 | ☐ | What are you reading?
3 | ☐ | Are you doing your homework?
4 | ☐ | Marie isn't coming with us. Why?
5 | ☐ | Are your friends swimming today?
6 | ☐ | Why is your teacher talking to Frank?

a He isn't working very hard.
b We're walking into town.
c No, they aren't. They're playing tennis.
d I'm looking at my friend's magazine.
e She's waiting for Mike.
f No, I'm writing a letter.

5 ●●● Complete the dialogue with the correct form of the verbs.

| not do ~~do~~ write watch play
| enjoy cook do

A: Hi! How are you?
B: I'm good, thanks. What ¹*are you doing*?
A: Not much. I'm at my computer.
B: ² _____ emails?
A: No, I'm not. I ³ _____ my History homework. And you?
B: Well, I ⁴ _____ my homework! I ⁵ _____ a reality show on TV with my brother, Ben.
A: ⁶ _____ the show?
B: No, I'm not. It's boring. Mum ⁷ _____ dinner and I haven't got time to start my homework.
A: It's hard! And Timmy ⁸ _____ his guitar in his room – he's really loud! I can't think!
B: I know, let's do our homework in the library.
A: That's a great idea!

I can find specific detail in a letter and talk about feelings.

1 Match comments 1–8 with descriptions a–h.

1 [c] I don't sleep very well.
2 [ ] This book isn't interesting at all!
3 [ ] I can hear a terrible noise outside.
4 [ ] My computer isn't working – again!
5 [ ] My dad is wearing a pink shirt!
6 [ ] We're going on holiday.
7 [ ] I can't find my dog!
8 [ ] I'm just sitting in the sun with my book.

a I'm worried.
b I'm embarrassed.
c I'm tired.
d It's boring.
e I'm relaxed.
f It's annoying.
g I'm frightened.
h It's exciting.

2 Choose the correct option.

1 When my mum tells a joke it's *embarrassed* / (*embarrassing*)!
2 James works from 6.30 until 7.30 in the evening. He's always *tired* / *tiring*.
3 My sister often takes my clothes without asking. I get very *annoying* / *annoyed*.
4 I love the new TV series. It's really *interested* / *interesting*.
5 Pam is *excited* / *exciting* about the concert tonight.
6 Jake doesn't like horror films. He gets *frightening* / *frightened* when he watches one.

3 Read the magazine interview with a famous actor and choose the correct answers.

1 At the moment Katy
   a is working.
   b is reading a magazine.
   (c) isn't doing anything.
2 Anna is from
   a a newspaper.
   b a magazine.
   c a TV company.
3 Katy usually lives
   a in the USA.
   b in the UK.
   c in Scotland.
4 Katy is in the UK
   a to work.
   b for a holiday.
   c to buy a house.
5 Newspapers show annoying pictures when
   a Katy isn't very well.
   b Katy isn't wearing make-up.
   c Katy is with her dog.

Interviewer: Hi, Katy. I'm Anna. Thank you for agreeing to do this interview.
Katy: That's OK. I have a day off and I'm just relaxing so I can talk to you. You're not interrupting anything!
Interviewer: That's good. I have some questions for you from our readers.
Katy: Cool! I really like your magazine.
Interviewer: Great! So, the first question is – do you usually work in the USA or in the UK?
Katy: Well, as you know, I live in Los Angeles in the States but I often come to the UK for work. I'm here right now to film a new TV show. Then I plan to have a short holiday in Scotland before I go back home.

Interviewer: Excellent! You're a very famous actor and our readers want to know – do you like being famous? Does anything annoy you?
Katy: That's a very good question! I love my work but some things about it are annoying! Often when I'm eating in a restaurant people ask for my autograph. Also, there's another thing I really hate. If I'm shopping in the supermarket and I'm not wearing smart clothes or make-up, photographers love it! They take a photograph and the next day it's in the newspaper with the words. 'Poor Katy is looking ill and tired! Is she working too hard?'
Interviewer: Well, you're definitely not looking tired or ill at the moment! Thank you, Katy.

I can talk about what usually happens and is happening around now.

1 ● Decide if the verbs in the sentences show facts (F), a routine (R), something happening during a period of time (P), or something happening right now (N).

1 [F] My mum works in a hospital.
2 [ ] She always gets up at 6.30 and takes a taxi to work.
3 [ ] Today she isn't feeling very well, so she's staying at home.
4 [ ] At the moment she's sitting in bed and sending some emails.
5 [ ] She has friends in lots of different countries.
6 [ ] She's working with a new team of doctors this week.
7 [ ] She usually finishes work at 6.00.
8 [ ] Oh dear – the phone is ringing. Perhaps it's the hospital.

2 ● Complete the sentences with the correct present form of the verbs.

1 I usually have cereal for breakfast. Today, I'*m having* some toast too.
2 Denny doesn't always come to extra Maths classes after school. He _____ this week because his marks are getting worse!
3 It always _____ when I'm on holiday and look – it's raining now!
4 I know you play tennis very often. _____ this week?
5 My friend _____ very near and she walks to school every morning.
6 My brother usually watches game shows but tonight he _____ a soap opera.

3 ●● Match the parts of the sentences.

1 [c] Cathy doesn't usually go to bed late
2 [ ] She really enjoys soap operas
3 [ ] She knows a lot of languages
4 [ ] She usually goes on holiday to other countries
5 [ ] She sometimes plays the guitar in a band
6 [ ] She doesn't often go out during the week

a but she hates game shows.
b but she's staying in London this week.
c but she's watching a film right now and it's already midnight!
d but this week she's playing the drums.
e but she's watching a film at the cinema with us right now.
f but she doesn't speak Italian.

4 ●● Choose the correct option.

1 We *usually study* / are usually studying Maths on Mondays but today we *have* / *'re having* a test.
2 Jenna's listening to some music *and* / *but* she's watching TV at the same time! How?
3 I *don't do* / *'m not doing* my homework at the moment because my computer *doesn't work* / *isn't working*.
4 Harry is waiting for Lisa outside school *and* / *but* she doesn't want to see him.
5 *Do you always have* / *Are you always having* a big breakfast before school? No, I *don't* / *'m not*.
6 My sister *usually wears* / *is usually wearing* jeans and a T-shirt *and* / *but* today she *wears* / *'s wearing* a smart skirt and jacket.

5 ●●● Complete the text with the correct form of the verbs.

play   sing x2   not get   hear
love   ~~have~~   enjoy   practise

● ● ●

My friend, Mia, is amazing. She's only fifteen but she [1]*has* a brilliant weekend job. Every Friday and Saturday night she [2]_____ with a band. She's got a lovely voice. Her brother [3]_____ the guitar. They're both really good musicians. They [4]_____ a lot of money but they [5]_____ it. The band always [6]_____ in our classroom during the lunch break and I can [7]_____ them now. Mia [8]_____ an Ellie Goulding song and it's beautiful! I [9]_____ their music!

I can identify specific detail in a conversation and talk about personality.

1 Complete the words from the descriptions.

1 This describes someone who shows their feelings: **o**utgoing

2 This describes someone who only thinks about himself: **s** _ _ _ _ _ _

3 This describes someone who likes telling people what to do: **b** _ _ _ _

4 This describes someone who is not polite: **r** _ _ _ _

5 This describes someone who thinks he's good at everything: **b** _ _ _ – _ _ _ _ _ _ _

6 This describes someone who is always happy: **c** _ _ _ _ _ _ _

2 Match pictures 1–5 with the adjectives.

| moody   polite   ~~hard-working~~   talkative   tidy

1 *hard-working* 2 _____ 3 _____

4 _____ 5 _____

3 Find the adjectives in the word search.

| quiet   shy   untidy   lazy   chatty   ~~helpful~~

H	E	L	P	F	U	L	G
F	E	P	D	M	N	O	Q
Q	C	H	A	T	T	Y	U
U	W	B	E	J	I	S	I
L	A	R	E	Z	D	H	E
E	S	L	A	Z	Y	Y	T

4 Complete the sentences with adjectives from Exercise 3.

1 Sara doesn't talk very much. She's very *quiet* .

2 Gary's very _____ . He's checking my computer at the moment because it isn't working very well.

3 My young sister is quite _____ and she doesn't like meeting new people.

4 I think I'm _____ ! I can talk about anything!

5 Don't look in my brother's room. It's a mess. He is so _____ .

6 I'm feeling _____ today. I don't want to do anything.

5 🔊 04 Listen to dialogues 1–5 and choose the correct answers.

1 Who is the boy's sister?
   a Anna   ⓑ Sally   c Alex

2 Where are the speakers?
   a in town   b in a café
   c in the park

3 When is the girl's party?
   a Wednesday   b Friday   c Saturday

4 What is Grace wearing to the concert?
   a a dress   b jeans   c trainers

5 What is Tim doing?
   a eating his breakfast
   b dancing at a club
   c sleeping in bed

6 🔊 04 Listen to the dialogues again. Mark the sentences true (T) or false (F).

1 _F_ (Dialogue 1) The new student is in Class 4.

2 ☐ (Dialogue 2) It isn't raining at the moment.

3 ☐ (Dialogue 3) The boy is giving the girl her birthday present now.

4 ☐ (Dialogue 4) The concert is in the school.

5 ☐ (Dialogue 4) The students are planning to go to the concert by car.

6 ☐ (Dialogue 5) Tim watches TV late on Fridays.

I can give and respond to news.

1 Match the parts of the sentences.

1	[e]	I'm learning
2	[ ]	My family is moving
3	[ ]	Our teacher's waiting
4	[ ]	I'm acting
5	[ ]	We're having
6	[ ]	I'm feeling very

a in the classroom.
b in the school play.
c tired this morning.
d lots of tests at the moment.
e how to play the piano.
f to a new house today.

2 Make sentences about giving news.

1 my sister / enjoy / her new job
My sister is enjoying her new job.

2 I / learn / a new language

_____

3 my mum / not feel well / these days

_____

4 I / spend a lot of money / at the moment / !

_____

5 the tennis tournament / go well

_____

6 my dad / feel / worried because he / have problems / with his new car

_____

3 🔊 05 Complete the responses with one word in each gap. Then listen and check.

| Poor kidding pity N̶o̶ That's Good done |

1 A: Dave's going out with Kim!
 B: *No* way!

2 A: My Maths results are brilliant!
 B: Well _____ !

3 A: My dog's ill.
 B: What a _____ !

4 A: This new shirt has got a hole in it.
 B: _____ terrible!

5 A: I've got lots of homework.
 B: _____ you!

6 A: I'm learning Mandarin Chinese!
 B: _____ for you!

7 A: We don't have any classes today!
 B: You're _____ !

4 Complete the table with the phrases from Exercise 3.

Good news	Bad news	Surprising news
Awesome!		*Amazing!*

5 Choose the correct answers.

1 I've got free tickets for the concert!
 a What a pity!
 (b) Awesome!
 c Poor you!

2 I can't go to Mike's party.
 a Amazing!
 b What a pity!
 c Good for you!

3 My dad's got a job in China.
 a Well done!
 b No way!
 c Good for you!

4 They're cutting down those lovely trees in Forest Road.
 a You're kidding!
 b Cool!
 c Poor you!

5 I'm feeling really ill today.
 a Well done!
 b Cool!
 c That's terrible!

I can talk about when something happens.

1 Complete the table with the words below.

> night   autumn   2018   my birthday
> ~~the morning~~   Easter   3.45   Sundays
> Monday morning   the weekend

IN	ON	AT
the morning		

2 Choose the correct option.

1 We always go out *in* / *on* Friday evenings and come back home *on* / *at* 11.30 *at* / *in* night.

2 I want to start a Zumba class *at* / *in* August but there aren't any classes *in* / *on* the summer because everyone is on holiday then.

3 We usually take our dog for a walk three times every day – *in* / *at* the morning, *in* / *at* the evening and *in* / *at* night.

4 *At* / *On* school days I get up *on* / *at* 7.30 but *on* / *at* the weekend I stay in bed later and *on* / *at* Sundays I get up *on* / *at* 12.00!

5 *In* / *At* Christmas my family stays with my grandparents and then we have a big party *at* / *on* New Year's Eve. It finishes *on* / *at* 3.00 *in* / *at* the morning!

6 My birthday's *at* / *in* summer, *at* / *on* 8 July. If it's *in* / *on* Saturday or Sunday I go swimming with my friends. I always get some money from my aunt and uncle *at* / *on* my birthday.

3 Complete the text with the correct prepositions.

> ¹*At* the moment my dad works ²_____ an office ³_____ Mondays, Wednesdays and Thursdays, starting ⁴_____ 5.30 every day. My mum works ⁵_____ the evenings. But they also have a clothes shop – my dad works there ⁶_____ Tuesdays and Fridays and my mum during the rest of the week. I sometimes work there ⁷_____ the weekend and ⁸_____ Wednesday afternoons when we don't have school. Of course, ⁹_____ the summer I can work there all the time! Fun – huh?!

4 🔊 06 Listen to an announcement and complete the information about the TwoTrees Shopping Centre.

🌳 **TwoTrees**
SHOPPING CENTRE

Opens on ¹*Saturday 14 August*
See Bruce Downton at ²_____
Blue Friday are playing in ³_____
Children's party at ⁴_____

Open all year but closed on ⁵_____

For each learning objective, tick (✓) the box that best matches your ability.

😊😊 = I understand and can help a friend.   ☹ = I understand but have some questions.

😊 = I understand and can do it by myself.   ☹☹ = I do not understand.

		😊😊	😊	☹	☹☹	Need help?	Now try ...
2.1	Vocabulary					Students' Book pp. 22–23 Workbook pp. 18–19	Ex. 1–2, p. 27
2.2	Grammar					Students' Book p. 24 Workbook p. 20	Ex. 3–5, p. 27
2.3	Reading					Students' Book p. 25 Workbook p. 21	
2.4	Grammar					Students' Book p. 26 Workbook p. 22	
2.5	Listening					Students' Book p. 27 Workbook p. 23	
2.6	Speaking					Students' Book p. 28 Workbook p. 24	Ex. 6, p. 27
2.7	English in Use					Students' Book p. 29 Workbook p. 25	

2.1   I can talk about clothes and appearance.
2.2   I can talk about present activities.
2.3   I can find specific detail in a letter and talk about feelings.
2.4   I can talk about what usually happens and is happening around now.
2.5   I can identify specific detail in a conversation and talk about personality.
2.6   I can give and respond to news.
2.7   I can talk about when something happens.

What can you remember from this unit?

New words I learned (the words you most want to remember from this unit)	**Expressions and phrases I liked** (any expressions or phrases you think sound nice, useful or funny)	**English I heard or read outside class** (e.g. from websites, books, adverts, films, music)

Vocabulary

1 Complete the sentences with the correct words.

> baggy belt pyjamas scarf
> tattoo trainers

1 I wear striped _____ to bed.
2 After football my _____ are always dirty.
3 I like the rose _____ on your arm.
4 Helen usually wears _____ T-shirts in the summer.
5 I need a tight _____ for these jeans.
6 When it's cold, my brother wears a red woolly _____ .

2 Complete the words in the sentences.

1 My sister always leaves her clothes on the floor. She's very **u**_____ .
2 I'm enjoying this book. It's **i**_____ .
3 Becky is always smiling. She's **c**_____ .
4 I don't like this horror film. It's **f**_____ .
5 I can't find my dog. I'm **w**_____ .
6 My brother tells bad jokes. He's very **i**_____ .

Grammar

3 Complete the sentences with the correct Present Continuous form of the verb in brackets.

1 Jacky _____ (wear) a blue skirt today.
2 Where _____ (Mike/go)?
3 I _____ (not do) Exercise 3. I _____ (do) Exercise 2.
4 **A:** _____ (Dan/drive) his dad's car?
   B: Yes, he _____ .
5 John _____ (not work). He _____ (sleep)!
6 Who _____ (you phone)?

4 Choose the correct option.

To: hello@evasmail.com

Hi Eva,

What ¹*are you doing / do you do*? I'm sure you ²*'re reading / read* a book. You ³*are reading / read* every evening!

I ⁴*'m sitting / sit* in my room at the moment. I ⁵*'m trying / try* to choose a dress to wear for the party tonight. I ⁶*'m not wanting / don't want* to wear the red one. I ⁷*'m always wearing / always wear* that one to parties I usually ⁸*am wearing / wear* my black shoes too. I need to buy some new clothes! ⁹*Are you wanting / Do you want* to come shopping with me on Saturday?

Anyway – see you later!

Jess

5 Complete the sentences with the correct prepositions.

1 My birthday is _____ April.
2 Our English class is _____ 10.30.
3 I go swimming _____ Thursdays.
4 We often play football _____ the weekend.
5 We always have a family party _____ Christmas Day.
6 Our teacher goes to Spain _____ the summer.

Speaking language practice

6 Choose the best replies.

1 I'm doing well at school.
   a Good for you!
   b What a pity!
2 My computer isn't working.
   a Amazing!
   b Poor you!
3 We've got a lovely new dog.
   a Awesome!
   b That's terrible!
4 It's raining again.
   a You're kidding!
   b Well done!
5 I've got a new expensive laptop!
   a What a pity!
   b No way!

1 Match the words and phrases 1–4 with photos A–D.

1 [C] a hipster   3 [ ] lace
2 [ ] high heels   4 [ ] a brand

2 Match words 1–4 with definitions a–d.

1 [a] vintage   3 [ ] layers
2 [ ] neat   4 [ ] well-fitting

a from a long time ago
b when you put things on top of other things
c tidy, smart
d not baggy or tight

3 Complete the sentences with the correct form of the words from Exercises 1 and 2.

1 The dress has beautiful *lace* on the skirt.
2 Jacky's clothes are always _____ with no marks or anything out of place.
3 I often go shopping to markets to find interesting old, _____ clothes.
4 My dad likes _____ suits that are both comfortable and smart.
5 When it's cold, wear _____ of clothes.
6 I can't understand why my friend wears very _____ – they must hurt her feet.
7 Famous _____ are always very expensive.
8 _____ love the art shop in our road.

4 Complete the words in the sentences.

1 A **trend** is something fashionable now.
2 The **a** _ _ _ _ _ _ _ _ are the people who watch a show.
3 When you **c** _ _ _ _, you hit your hands together to show that you like a performance.
4 Models walk along a **c** _ _ _ _ _ _ _.

5 Match verbs 1–5 with phrases a–e to make Word Friends.

1 [e] style   a snacks
2 [ ] eat   b your nails
3 [ ] take   c a photograph
4 [ ] do   d your make-up
5 [ ] paint   e your hair

6 Complete the sentences with the correct form of the Word Friends from Exercise 5.

1 My sister likes to *paint her nails* bright red.
2 My mum _____ every day before work – she often puts blue on her eyes.
3 I never _____ during the day because I usually have a big lunch.
4 This magazine has got some interesting ways to _____ – there's advice for both long and short.
5 Come and _____ of us – then we can upload it to Facebook.

7 Look at the photos from the video. What are the people doing? Complete the sentences below.

1 The audience is *clapping*.
2 The male model is _____.
3 The models are _____.
4 The man is _____.
5 The woman is _____.
6 The man is _____.

8 Read the video script. Underline any words or phrases you don't know and find their meaning in your dictionary.

London Fashion Week
Part 1

Most people like fashion and buying new clothes but how do you know what's fashionable this year? You can look in magazines but if you want to know the latest trends, go to London Fashion Week or
5 watch it on TV.

There are two London Fashion Weeks every year – in February and September. More than 5,000 people go to see the new designs. They are reporters, buyers from shops, as well as people like you and me. They spend millions of pounds!
10 The models walk along a catwalk between the people. The audience watch the models and look at the different clothes. Here you can see that some people are taking photographs and others are taking notes. They're probably from magazines and newspapers. The models are wearing different types of clothes but
15 they are all interesting. There's music too and it's exciting. At the end of the show, all the models come onto the catwalk together and the audience claps as they go past. We can see the different styles and colours. There are dresses and shorts, baggy clothes and tight clothes, clothes for the day and clothes for the
20 night.

Some models are wearing high heels and some are wearing flat shoes or no shoes at all. But one thing is always the same – the clothes are all very expensive.

We usually think these shows are for women but there are men's
25 shows too. The men usually walk round like the women but at this event there's a difference. They're walking and … dancing. It's surprising! Some of them are good dancers and some are not so good! What do you think?

Part 2

30 When we watch the show, the models are perfect but it isn't easy to look like that. The clothes are ready but the models are not! They must look very good. Their pictures will be in lots of magazines! There are lots of people to help them. There are people to do their make-up … and paint their nails. And of course there's a
35 hairdresser to style their hair. While they get ready, they talk and laugh. It's a good, interesting job.

The models here are enjoying some food. They need a lot of energy for the show. They have to change clothes very often and very quickly in one show. While they're waiting in the dressing room,
40 there are lots of lovely snacks to eat.

Finally it's time to go on the catwalk – but first a photograph with perfect hair, perfect make-up and perfect clothes!

Animal magic

3

VOCABULARY
Animals | Animal body parts | Personality

GRAMMAR
Past Simple: *was/were* | Past Simple: regular verbs

READING
An article about orangutans | Right / wrong / doesn't say

LISTENING
Matching sentences and pictures | Matching dialogues and pictures

SPEAKING
Apologising

WRITING
A biography

BBC CULTURE
Why do parrots talk?

EXAM TIME 1 > p. 114

I can talk about animals.

1 ● Complete the names of the animals.

1 s h a_rk_
2 b u _ _ _ _ _ _ y
3 s p _ _ _ _ r
4 g i _ _ _ _ e
5 k a _ _ _ _ _ _ o
6 s n _ _ e
7 m o _ _ _ _ y
8 c h _ _ _ _ _ n

2 ● Find the animals from Exercise 1 in the word search.

C	S	C	A	I	J	T	H	X	B	E	Y
H	V	W	A	A	E	Y	T	Y	O	E	P
I	O	C	L	T	F	S	L	O	K	S	N
C	G	I	R	A	F	F	E	N	P	N	E
K	A	N	G	A	R	O	O	F	N	Z	A
E	X	H	E	E	N	M	M	S	D	U	X
N	S	S	T	M	T	J	T	P	T	X	Y
S	V	T	B	W	S	F	X	I	L	S	E
O	U	H	C	Y	N	H	O	D	E	H	R
B	H	S	N	O	A	D	A	E	P	S	C
D	U	R	I	V	K	M	E	R	X	L	Q
S	R	O	T	S	E	C	D	B	K	L	S

3 ● Decide if the animals below are farm animals (F), wild animals (W) or insects (I).

1 W tiger
2 ☐ bear
3 ☐ ant
4 ☐ sheep
5 ☐ chimp
6 ☐ donkey
7 ☐ duck
8 ☐ chicken
9 ☐ spider
10 ☐ dolphin
11 ☐ cow
12 ☐ bee
13 ☐ monkey
14 ☐ fly
15 ☐ butterfly

4 ●● Match descriptions 1–8 with animals a–h.

1 g It's very slow.
2 ☐ It's black and white.
3 ☐ It lives in the sea.
4 ☐ It visits flowers.
5 ☐ It's very, very big.
6 ☐ It gives us milk.
7 ☐ It can sometimes talk.
8 ☐ It has very long ears.

a parrot
b cow
c rabbit
d zebra
e dolphin
f bee
g tortoise
h elephant

5 ● Choose the correct answers.

1 Which animal doesn't have a tail?
   (a) butterfly   b rabbit   c zebra
2 Which animal doesn't have fur?
   a snake   b chimp   c tiger
3 Which animal doesn't have wings?
   a bee   b dolphin   c parrot
4 Which animal doesn't have feathers?
   a duck   b parrot   c ant
5 Which animal doesn't have claws?
   a rabbit   b cow   c bear

6 ●● Complete the sentences with the correct words.

| tails   wings x2   ~~feathers~~   claws   fur |

1 Parrots have brightly coloured *feathers*.
2 Monkeys use their _____ to hold onto trees when they jump.
3 Bears have different coloured _____. Sometimes it's brown, sometimes white and sometimes black.
4 Ducks have _____ and can fly when they want to.
5 Our dog has long _____ and we have to cut them from time to time.
6 The _____ of a butterfly are usually very pretty.

7 ●● Choose the correct option.

1 A bee *swims* / (*flies*) and has *wings* / *claws*.
2 A duck *climbs* / *swims* and has *claws* / *feathers*.
3 A monkey *climbs* / *flies* and has *feathers* / *a tail*.
4 A tiger eats *vegetables* / *meat* and has *wings* / *claws*.
5 A rabbit *jumps* / *swims* and has *feathers* / *fur*.
6 A shark *walks* / *bites* and lives in the *forest* / *sea*.

8 ●●● Complete the email with the correct words.

| ducks   rabbits   ~~butterflies~~   sheep
| tails   wings   tortoise   claws |

To: emma@fastmessage.com

Hi Emma,

When you're on holiday in Lyndhurst you must visit the Wildlife Centre. It's brilliant. They have a special room for beautiful ¹*butterflies*. They have very pretty ²_____ and there are hundreds of them flying all over the place. Sometimes they land on your arm or head! If you have your young sister with you, she can go to the pets' farm. They usually have some baby animals there. She can pick up the baby ³_____ – their mothers are out in the field with their long woolly coats eating grass! And there are a lot of ⁴_____ with their little round white fluffy ⁵_____. She can pick them up but be careful because their ⁶_____ can be quite sharp! If you want a new pet, you can buy one to take home! The centre also sells their wooden houses to keep in the garden. The baby ⁷_____ are really cute too. They follow their mother in a long line to the river for a swim! And there's a ⁸_____ that is nearly a hundred years old at the centre too! It lives in a warm box in the winter but in the summer you can see it walking very, very slowly across the grass!

Have fun!

Chris

I can use *was* and *were* to talk about the past.

1 ● **Complete the sentences with** *was, wasn't, were* **and** *weren't*.

1 I *wasn't* at school last week because I _____ on holiday with my parents.

2 We _____ in Spain, on the south coast.

3 We _____ in a very expensive hotel because dad wanted a cheap holiday! But it _____ nice and there _____ a lot of teenagers there – cool for me!

4 Our hotel _____ on the beach and I _____ in the water every day!

5 It _____ very hot but the sea _____ quite warm and good for swimming.

6 There _____ an aquarium near the hotel and there _____ some interesting fish! There _____ any sharks or dolphins – just small fish.

2 ● **Order the words to make questions.**

1 after / you / football / tired / yesterday / were / ?
Were you tired after football yesterday?

2 your / party / were / at / the / friends / ?
_____

3 morning / Marie / class / was / this / in / ?
_____

4 open / evening / shops / were / yesterday / the / ?
_____

5 the / interesting / film / was / ?
_____

6 house / Tim / last / was / night / your / at / ?
_____

3 ● **Write short answers for the questions in Exercise 2.**

1 Yes, *I was*.

2 No, _____ .

3 Yes, _____ .

4 Yes, _____ .

5 No, _____ .

6 No, _____ .

4 ● **Choose the correct option.**

1 I was in England (in) / *at* the summer.

2 We were *in* / *at* the cinema *at* / *on* Saturday.

3 I was *at* / *on* home this morning.

4 Were you *at* / *in* Rob's party?

5 They weren't *in* / *at* the classroom *on* / *at* 9.15. It was empty.

6 The dog was *at* / *in* the park this afternoon.

5 ●● **Read the sentences and make questions about the underlined words.**

1 We were in Switzerland <u>last week</u>.
When were you in Switzerland?

2 They were <u>in the park</u> at lunchtime.
_____

3 I was with <u>Janey</u> after school.
_____

4 The weather was <u>hot</u> in Italy.
_____

5 The film was on TV <u>at 7.30</u>.
_____

6 <u>Jake</u> was on the phone.
_____

6 ●●● **Complete the dialogue with the correct words.**

A: Hi! [1]*Where* were you after school? You [2]_____ at the café.

B: No, I [3]_____ . I was [4]_____ the park with my dog. The weather [5]_____ lovely. There [6]_____ a lot of rabbits and she was very happy! [7]_____ Mark at the café?

A: Yes, he [8]_____ . He was with Sally from Class 5. Later they [9]_____ at the cinema together too! I was there with Jenny.

B: [10]_____ was the film?

A: *True Love!*

B: Ahhh! [11]_____ it good?

A: It [12]_____ very good but Mark and Sally were happy. 'True Love' I think!

I can find specific detail in an article and talk about behaviour.

1 Complete the words from the descriptions.

1 This is someone who can't remember things: **f**orgetful

2 This is someone who is cute and other people like a lot: **l** _ _ _ _ _ _

3 This is someone who gets angry and sometimes fights: **a** _ _ _ _ _ _ _ _

4 This is someone who likes doing new and dangerous things: **a** _ _ _ _ _ _ _ _ _

5 This is someone who does things quickly without thinking: **i** _ _ _ _ _ _ _ _ _

2 Read the text. Mark the sentences right (✓), wrong (✗), or doesn't say (?).

1 [?] All animals need to live with both parents for a short time.

2 [ ] There are some similarities between orangutan and human babies.

3 [ ] The orangutans' home is disappearing.

4 [ ] At school baby orangutans learn different subjects to humans.

5 [ ] Orangutans know naturally the right food they should eat.

6 [ ] Orphaned orangutans always return to the jungle.

7 [ ] The International Animal Rescue charity can't save all the orphans.

3 Complete the definitions with the correct words from the text.

| jungle   nest   orphaned   ~~instinct~~   volunteer
| charity   survive   enormous

1 When we know something without learning it: *instinct*

2 An adjective to describe something that is very big: _____

3 An adjective to describe a person without parents: _____

4 A thick, tropical forest: _____

5 An organisation that helps people or animals: _____

6 To manage to live: _____

7 A home or safe place, often in the trees: _____

8 A person who does a job for no money: _____

4 Match words 1–6 with words a–f to make Word Friends.

1 [c] belong   a dangerous things
2 [ ] come   b shy
3 [ ] do   c to gangs
4 [ ] ignore   d a lot of noise
5 [ ] make   e advice
6 [ ] feel   f home late

School for Orangutans!

Everyone needs to go to school. We need to learn things that can help us when we grow up. But what about animals?

People say that animals are born with instincts and know naturally how to survive. However, that is not exactly true. Animals depend a lot on their mothers, at least for a short time, to teach them different skills. So, what happens when they have no mothers? For many baby orangutans in Borneo this is an enormous problem. Young orangutans are like human babies because they stay with their mothers for a long time. They learn lots of skills from their mothers before they can live by themselves. But a lot of orangutans are dying in Borneo because people are cutting down the rainforests where they live. Babies are losing their mothers and it is impossible for them to survive. The charity International Animal Rescue tries to save them.

Today in Borneo there is a special school for orphaned baby orangutans! Volunteers teach them all the things they need to learn. At Baby School they learn how to climb trees, what to eat and where to build nests to sleep safely. The good students go on to Forest School and later they return to the jungle. Humans aren't the same as mother orangutans but they give these lovable babies a real chance to live.

I can use the Past Simple of regular verbs to talk about the past.

1 Complete the words in the expressions.

OUT of class

1 Don't be so angry. **C** _ _ _ down!
2 You look terrible. What's the **m** _ _ _ _ _?
3 You're crying. What's **w** _ _ _ _?

2 ● Complete the sentences with the past form of the verbs.

| help   walk   ~~want~~   arrive   decide   look

1 Olly _wanted_ to be a vet when he was younger.
2 Jack _____ me with my animal project last night.
3 We _____ at photos of Annie's cat this morning.
4 I _____ to take my sister Tilly to the zoo for her birthday.
5 Megan and Bree _____ late for class this morning.
6 The penguins at the zoo _____ in a funny way!

3 ● Complete the sentences with the negative form of the verbs.

1 I needed some paper. I _didn't need_ a pen.
2 Harry phoned Leo. He _____ me.
3 We studied vocabulary. We _____ grammar.
4 They walked on the beach. They _____ in the park.
5 Dad promised to get us a cat. He _____ to get us a dog.
6 We watched a film on TV. We _____ a DVD.

4 ● Order the words to make questions. Then write short answers.

1 you / did / yesterday / phone / he / ?
Did he phone you yesterday? Yes, _he did_.
2 answer / question / teacher's / you / the / did / ?
_____
No, _____.
3 walk / party / they / to / did / the / ?
_____
Yes, _____.
4 in / look / dress / I / my / did / new / OK / ?
_____
Yes, _____.
5 police / did / dog / look / the / for / the / ?
_____
No, _____.
6 the / at / finish / 9.30 / TV / did / programme / ?
_____
No, _____.

5 ●● Complete the dialogues with the correct Past Simple form of the verbs.

1 (watch)
A: _Did you watch_ the documentary about wild animals last night?
B: No, I _didn't watch_ the documentary but I _watched_ a game show.
2 (phone)
A: When _____ Hannah?
B: I _____ her at 7.30 but she wasn't at home.
3 (listen)
A: _____ to George Ezra's new song?
B: Yes, I _____ to it last night. It was brilliant.
4 (end)
A: When _____?
B: The film _____ after midnight! It was late.
5 (play)
A: What _____ at the concert?
B: The band _____ their new song. They only recorded it last month! But they _____ all their old ones.
6 (rain)
A: _____ while you were on holiday?
B: No, it _____. It was sunny every day.

6 ●●● Complete the dialogue with the correct form of the verbs.

| print   change   play   promise   ~~ask~~
not play   look   not finish   decide

A: Did you start the animal project last night?
B: Yes, I did. I [1]_asked_ Andy to help me.
A: But he [2]_____ tennis last night.
B: He [3]_____ his plans. He [4]_____ tennis. He [5]_____ to help me instead!
A: That was very kind of him!
B: I know. We [6]_____ online and [7]_____ some interesting articles about wildlife in Africa. We [8]_____ but he [9]_____ to help me again tonight.
A: Lucky you!

3.5 LISTENING and VOCABULARY   Pets

I can identify specific detail in a conversation and talk about pets.

1 WORD FRIENDS **Match the parts of the sentences. Then match sentences 1–6 with pictures A–F.**

1 d Cats often give   a our furniture and mum gets mad.
2 ☐ I brush   b my dog for a walk after school.
3 ☐ I have to empty   c your home.
4 ☐ I usually take   d people allergies.
5 ☐ Our cat scratches   e my dog's fur every day.
6 ☐ If you get a big dog, it can protect f our cat's litter tray because it smells!

2 🔊 **07 Listen to five short dialogues. Match dialogues 1–5 with pictures A–E.**

3 🔊 **07 Listen again and choose the correct answers.**

1 What does the dog, Harry, usually eat?
   (a) dog biscuits   b same food as the family   c chicken
2 What's the weather like?
   a it's raining   b it's cloudy   c it's sunny
3 How many lions were there when the boy was at the park?
   a none   b two   c four
4 What did the girl NOT do?
   a give food to the cat b empty the cat's litter tray   c put water in the cat's bowl
5 What is the girl's gran's new pet?
   a a cat   b a tortoise   c a parrot

I can make and respond to apologies.

1 **Complete the table with the phrases below.**

> It's all my fault.   Never mind.
> I totally understand.   I'm so sorry.
> You can't be serious!   I'll never forgive you!
> These things happen.
> How could you be so careless?
> I'm really angry about this.   No problem.

Apologising	Accepting apologies	Not accepting apologies
I apologise.	It's not your fault.	You promised to.
I feel terrible.		
It was an accident.		
It's all my fault.		

2 **Choose the correct responses.**

1   I'm sorry I'm late.
   a   Good for you!
   b   Here you are.
   c   No problem.

2   I'm sorry – I dropped your book in the bath.
   a   Oh, come on, please!
   b   It's all my fault.
   c   These things happen.

3   I'm sorry I didn't remember to bring your DVD.
   a   Never mind.
   b   Here you are.
   c   Well done.

4   I'm sorry I knocked your tortoise off the table.
   a   That's amazing!
   b   What's wrong?
   c   How could you be so careless!

5   I'm sorry I burned the dinner.
   a   I don't get it!
   b   These things happen.
   c   How much is that?

3 🔊 **08** **Complete the dialogues with one word in each gap. Listen and check.**

1   A: I'm sorry. I've got tickets for the wrong concert. I *feel* terrible.
   B: You can't be _____ . They were really expensive!

2   A: I'm sorry I didn't finish my homework last night.
   B: _____ mind. You can give it in tomorrow.

3   A: I'm really late for the meeting. I _____ .
   B: No _____ . Jane's not here yet.

4   A: I'm sorry but I have to leave early. I need to go to the dentist.
   B: I _____ understand.

5   A: Oops! I deleted your file. Sorry – it was an _____ .
   B: How could you be so _____ ? Now I've got to write it all again.

6   A: I'm really sorry. I showed Tommy a photo of you and your French boyfriend in the summer.
   B: You can't be _____ ! I'll never _____ you!

I can write a biography.

1 Read a short biography of Jane Goodall and answer the questions.

1 Which animals is she interested in?
2 Where did she study in 1962?

myblog

Jane Goodall

A

Jane Goodall is a ¹*famous* wildlife expert and writer. She is especially interested in monkeys and chimps.

B

She was ²_____ in 1934. She ³_____ in London with her parents. When she was a child she received a toy chimpanzee from her parents. This started her love for monkeys.

C

In 1958 she ⁴_____ with wild chimps in Tanzania and watched their behaviour and actions. She decided to study at Cambridge University in 1962. She then ⁵_____ to Tanzania and continued studying chimps.

D

Jane studied chimps for fifty-five years. In 1977 she ⁶_____ an organisation to protect wild chimpanzees. She still ⁷_____ to protect wild animals today.

2 Now complete the biography with the correct words.

| works lived returned born ~~famous~~
| worked started

3 Match topics 1-4 with paragraphs A–D in the biography.

1 Early career C
2 Childhood and family ___
3 Later life ___
4 Reason she is famous ___

4 Complete the information in the fact box about Steve Backshall.

| karate ~~TV presenter~~ 2014 British Airways
| five Colombian *Tiger Wars* 1973 Biology

Name:	Steve Backshall
Reason he's famous:	naturalist, writer and ¹*TV presenter*
Born:	²_____
Childhood:	parents worked for ³_____, many holidays in exotic countries
Studies:	Theatre and English at Exeter, ⁴_____ at Open University, learned judo and ⁵_____ in Japan
Early career:	filmed trip in ⁶_____ jungle for TV, presenter on National Geographic Channel for ⁷_____ years
Later life:	published novel ⁸_____ in 2012, danced in TV competition 'Strictly Come Dancing' in ⁹_____ still popular today

5 Use the fact box to write a short biography (70–100 words) about Steve Backshall.

a Divide the information into four paragraphs:
 1 Reason he is famous
 2 Childhood and family
 3 Early career
 4 Later life
b Use the text in Exercise 1 as a model.
c Use the Past Simple in the blog.

For each learning objective, tick (✓) the box that best matches your ability.

☺☺ = I understand and can help a friend.   ☹ = I understand but have some questions.

☺ = I understand and can do it by myself.   ☹☹ = I do not understand.

		☺☺	☺	☹	☹☹	Need help?	Now try ...
3.1	Vocabulary					Students' Book pp. 34–35 Workbook pp. 30–31	Ex. 1–3, p. 39
3.2	Grammar					Students' Book p. 36 Workbook p. 32	Ex. 4–5, p. 39
3.3	Reading					Students' Book p. 37 Workbook p. 33	
3.4	Grammar					Students' Book p. 38 Workbook p. 34	
3.5	Listening					Students' Book p. 39 Workbook p. 35	
3.6	Speaking					Students' Book p. 40 Workbook p. 36	Ex. 6, p. 39
3.7	Writing					Students' Book p. 41 Workbook p. 37	

3.1   I can talk about animals.
3.2   I can use *was* and *were* to talk about the past.
3.3   I can find specific detail in an article and talk about behaviour.
3.4   I can use the Past Simple of regular verbs to talk about the past.
3.5   I can identify specific detail in a conversation and talk about pets.
3.6   I can make and respond to apologies.
3.7   I can write a biography.

What can you remember from this unit?

New words I learned (the words you most want to remember from this unit)	**Expressions and phrases I liked** (any expressions or phrases you think sound nice, useful or funny)	**English I heard or read outside class** (e.g. from websites, books, adverts, films, music)

Vocabulary

1 Circle the odd one out.

1 **Insects:**
spider   snake   ant

2 **Farm animals:**
cow   sheep   bear

3 **Water animals:**
monkey   dolphin   shark

4 **Large animals:**
giraffe   duck   elephant

5 **Flying animals:**
butterfly   rabbit   parrot

6 **Animal skin:**
fur   feather   claw

2 Complete the sentences with the correct adjectives.

> adventurous aggressive careless
> forgetful impulsive shy

1 Someone who likes to fight and shout is _____ .

2 Someone who doesn't like talking or meeting people is _____ .

3 Someone who can't remember things is_____ .

4 Someone who does things without thinking for a long time is _____ .

5 Someone who likes trying new things is _____ .

6 Someone who isn't careful is

_____ .

3 Choose the correct option.

1 A big dog can *protect* / *feed* your home.

2 I *take* / *brush* my dog's fur every day.

3 My brother's job is to *scratch* / *empty* his cat's litter tray in the morning.

4 Cats *make* / *give* my sister allergies.

5 Don't allow your pets to *brush* / *scratch* the furniture.

6 How often do you *go* / *take* your dog for a walk?

Grammar

4 Write sentences using the correct past form of *be*.

1 I / in bed early last night [✓]

_____

2 your parents / at the concert on Saturday [?]

_____

3 That programme / very interesting [✗]

_____

4 Tom / at your party [?]

_____

5 What / your favourite film last year [?]

_____

6 There / any monkeys at the safari park [✗]

_____

5 Complete the sentences using the correct past form of the verbs in brackets.

1 When I _____ (be) younger I _____ (not like) classical music.

2 Where _____ (you/live) before you _____ (move) here last year?

3 My dad _____ (not work) last month because he _____ (be) ill.

4 A: _____ (you/watch) the film on TV last night?
B: No, I _____ . We _____ (be) out.

5 I _____ (phone) you yesterday but you _____ (not answer). _____ (you/be) at the leisure centre?

6 _____ (the teacher/explain) some new grammar in class today? I _____ (be) at the doctor's.

Speaking language practice

6 Complete the dialogues with the correct words.

> accident all can't could feel
> forgive happen No so totally

1 A: I'm _____ sorry. It's _____ my fault.
B: Never mind. I _____ understand.

2 A: I _____ terrible.
B: _____ problem. These things _____ .

3 A: I apologise. It was an _____ .
B: How _____ you be so careless?

4 A: I'm really sorry.
B: You _____ be serious! I'll never _____ you!

1 Look at pages 44–45 of the Students' Book. Use the letters to write the correct words for animals which you see on those pages.

1 **SLIGHOFD** *goldfish*
2 **RROTAP** _____
3 **BRITBA** _____
4 **KEANS** _____
5 **STHARME** _____
6 **PYPPU** _____

2 Match the pairs of sentences.

1 [b] I'm a vegetarian.
2 [ ] I'm very lucky.
3 [ ] I have a bad memory.
4 [ ] I'm very gentle.
5 [ ] I have a poisonous pet.
6 [ ] I have an aggressive pet.

a Be careful! My dog might bite you.
b Sorry, I don't eat meat or fish.
c I always pick him up very carefully – I don't want to frighten him.
d I dropped my phone in the water and it still works!
e I didn't remember it was your birthday.
f These spiders are small but they can kill you!

3 Complete the sentences with words from Exercise 2.

1 This is my *lucky* coin – I always take it into exams with me.
2 Parts of this flower are _____, so don't touch them.
3 This puppy is friendly but his brother is very _____.
4 When someone invites me for dinner, I have to tell them that I'm a _____.
5 Please be _____ with the puppy because he's very young.
6 I have a bad _____ for names I'm afraid. Is your dog called Bailey or Marley?

4 Match items 1–4 with the places where you might find them a–d.

1 [d] cushions   a at a zoo
2 [ ] a cage   b in the bathroom
3 [ ] a wheel   c on a car
4 [ ] a mirror   d on a sofa

5 Complete the verbs from the descriptions.

1 To keep something in a safe place:
s t o r e
2 To copy what someone does or says:
_ i _ _ _ _
3 To run away: _ s _ _ _ _ _
4 To catch other animals for food:
_ u _ _
5 To get ready: _ r _ _ _ _ _ e

6 Complete the sentences with the correct prepositions.

| about   for x2   ~~into~~   in x2   from   on   to

1 Hamsters push food *into* their mouths.
2 The puppies are playing _____ the bed.
3 The hamster needs to escape _____ bigger animals.
4 Puppies fight to prepare _____ real life _____ the wild.
5 Puppies learn rules _____ working in a group.
6 Parrots sometimes talk _____ a mirror.
7 We keep some animals _____ cages.
8 Parrots don't just talk _____ fun. There's a reason for what they do.

7 Read the video script. Underline any words or phrases you don't know and find their meaning in your dictionary.

Wild at heart

We think we understand our pets. They're cute and lovable – our best friends. These puppies playing on the bed seem very different from wild dogs. We love to watch them play but are their games really just games? No,

5 there's an important reason for this behaviour. While they play, they're training to catch and eat smaller animals for food. Also, they need to practise working together. They need to be in a group to catch and kill big animals. Here they're learning the rules about working in a group. They

10 learn when to fight and when to stop. These puppies are only seven weeks old but in their game these cushions are small animals. Play prepares them for life in the wild. Dogs are not the only pets that practise real life skills. Hamsters are popular pets and in their cages, they run

15 round and round a special wheel. There's a reason for this too. In the wild they run a long way – sometimes ten kilometres – every day. Big animals hunt them and they need to escape.

But that's not the only amazing thing which hamsters

20 do. They push lots and lots of food into their mouths. It's nearly impossible! But why do they do this? In the wild, when they find food, they need to store it. Perhaps they won't find any for a long time. Their mouths are like cupboards! There's another reason too. When a big

25 animal is hunting them, they sometimes need to put their babies in their mouths … and run!

Some people keep birds in cages too. But birds don't like to be alone. They like to talk – sometimes to the mirror! Some birds are very clever and they can mimic us and

30 copy what people say to them!

But why do birds do this? Is it for fun?

"It's not easy being green."

Again, they're practising a skill which they need in the wild. Every group of birds uses different sounds – like a

35 different language.

"Never shake a baby bird. That would surely be absurd."

Birds need to talk the same language as their group. So, a parrot in a cage copies our words in order to practise this skill. It wants to become part of our group, our family.

40 It even talks to other pets! This bird, Disco, can say 130 words. Amazing, isn't it?

4

New technology

I can talk about technology.

1 ● Label photos 1–8 with the correct words.

| DVD player   smartphone   tablet   CD player   e-reader
| MP3 player   ~~digital camera~~   games console

digital camera _____   _____   _____

 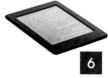 

2 ●● Complete the sentences with the correct words from Exercise 1.

1 My best present ever was a *games console*. It was very expensive but I play on it a lot with my friends.

2 My dad doesn't like my _____. He says he likes to turn over real pages!

3 I use my _____ to talk to my friends everywhere I go. I've got a cool ringtone too.

4 My aunt does not use her _____ anymore because she downloads all her music online.

5 I don't use my _____ much now, even though it's very small – I listen to my music on my smartphone or _____.

6 Mum and dad usually record films from TV on their _____ but I usually watch them later online.

7 My brother takes lots of photos and my dad got him a brilliant _____ for his birthday.

3 ● **WORD FRIENDS** Complete the words in the sentences.

1 I **l***isten* to music on my MP3 player.

2 I s __ r __ the internet on my tablet.

3 I t __ __ __ photos with my digital camera.

4 I r __ **a** __ novels on my e-reader.

5 I w __ t __ __ films on my DVD player.

6 I c __ __ **c** __ emails on my smartphone.

7 I m __ __ __ video clips on my computer.

8 I p __ **a** __ games on my games console.

4 ●● Match the parts of the sentences.

1 [_h_] I always listen
2 [ ] We're reading
3 [ ] My friend checks
4 [ ] My dad downloads
5 [ ] I like sending
6 [ ] My mum's phone doesn't take
7 [ ] Some friends and I made
8 [ ] After school I often surf

a a good novel in English lessons this term.
b the internet for hours.
c emails in class and the teacher gets angry with her.
d a video clip and put it on YouTube.
e files regularly for his work.
f instant messages because it's quick.
g photos because it's really old!
h to music when I'm travelling.

5 ● Complete the sentences with the correct words.

> ~~battery~~ pen drive USB ports memory
> keyboard joystick

1 I need to get a new _battery_ for my phone.
2 I can't read the letter 'E' on my _____ anymore!
3 The _____ for my games console is broken.
4 I haven't got enough _____ to download all the photos.
5 There are several _____ on my laptop – they're really useful.
6 How much is a _____? I'd like to store my photos on one.

6 ●● Choose the correct answers.

1 I use my ___ camera for taking very good photographs.
  a CD   b DVD   ⓒ digital
2 My friend is making a video ___ of her dog to post online.
  a memory b clip c text
3 My CD ___ isn't working and I can't listen to my favourite discs.
  a player b tablet c console
4 If your ___ is full, you can't download any more photos.
  a file b joystick c memory
5 You plug this into your ___ and then you can store files on it.
  a pen drive b battery c USB port
6 How often do you ___ your emails?
  a surf b check c watch

7 ●●● Complete the blog with the correct words.

My blog

ABOUT ME | **NEW POSTS** | CONTACT ME

 computerfan100 18.45pm

I guess I'm a computer freak! I'm always on my computer and I love my gadgets! When I wake up I [1]_check_ my emails and texts. While I'm having breakfast I listen to music on my MP3 player and send some instant [2]_____ to my best friend. I don't often phone her because it's quicker and easier to speak online! I have my [3]_____ in my pocket with me everywhere – even in class. I can go online and [4]_____ the internet for information – that's educational! At break and after school I [5]_____ games on my phone. In the evening I sometimes use the [6]_____ and watch a film on our big screen. I don't have many books because I read them on an [7]_____ and I keep all my photos on a really small [8]_____, which I keep in my pocket. At the end of the day my phone and tablet batteries are down, so I [9]_____ them before I go to bed. I cannot imagine living without my gadgets!

COMMENTS **0** LIKES 👍

I can use the Past Simple of irregular verbs to talk about the past.

1 ● Write the past tenses of the irregular verbs.

1 cost *cost*   5 forget _____
2 buy _____   6 go _____
3 lose _____   7 take _____
4 do _____   8 find _____

2 ● Find the irregular past tenses of the verbs in the word search.

> ~~eat~~ have put send leave do
> see get steal give

A	T	O	S	C	N	P	T	E	P
N	T	V	R	Q	A	U	G	Y	A
C	D	I	R	D	E	T	L	O	I
T	I	S	A	I	W	S	E	N	T
T	S	H	E	D	T	T	F	E	M
A	N	D	E	N	N	O	T	H	E
G	O	L	P	N	P	L	S	V	W
D	I	E	O	T	F	E	A	H	W
D	A	P	P	X	R	G	W	Z	Q
Z	I	G	T	C	S	C	E	R	N

3 ●● Complete the sentences with the past form of the verbs.

> put send steal cost ask ~~get~~
> forget see give

1 Harry *got* a new laptop for his birthday last month.
2 A thief _____ Rianna's phone, tablet and MP3 player during lunchbreak.
3 I _____ Katy some help in class today.
4 Sorry, I _____ to bring your book back today.
5 Dan _____ me three texts about the party last night!
6 My new watch _____ a lot of money but I love it.
7 I _____ Amy this morning and she _____ for your email address.
8 I'm sure I _____ my homework here on the table this morning. Where is it?

4 ●● Complete the dialogues with the correct form of the verbs.

1 **SEE**
A: I *saw* a new film yesterday.
B: Oh, _____ *Magic Men*?
A: No, I _____ *Magic Men*. I _____ *Heroes*.

2 **BUY**
A: Mum and dad _____ a new TV last week.
B: Oh, _____ a Samsung?
A: No, they _____ a Samsung. They _____ a Panasonic.

3 **GIVE**
A: The teacher _____ us a test in class today.
B: Oh, _____ you a long test?
A: No, she _____ us a long test. She _____ us a VERY long test!

4 **LEAVE**
A: Mack and Lily _____ school early today.
B: Oh, _____ after lunch?
A: No, they _____ after lunch. They _____ after Maths.

5 ●●● Use the prompts to complete the dialogue.

A: the new electronics store / open / yesterday; you / go?
> [1] *The new electronics store opened yesterday. Did you go?*

B: Yeah; I / go / with Tina; we / arrange / to meet for lunch
2 _____

A: where / you / go / ?
3 _____

B: we / find / a table / at Marco's
4 _____

A: what / you / have / ?
5 _____

B: I / have / pizza; Tina / not eat / anything; she / not be / hungry
6 _____

A: so, how many / gadgets / you / buy / ?
7 _____

B: I / not buy / any / ! / we / not stay / long; it / be / very crowded / !
8 _____

I can find specific detail in a text and talk about using technology.

1 PHRASAL VERBS Complete the advice with the correct verbs.

Look   switch   ~~keep~~   Hang   Check   give

1 A: Lovely to see you! Goodbye!
   B: Please *keep* in touch.

2 A: My computer isn't working!
   B: Did you _____ it on?

3 A: Someone keeps calling me and never says anything!
   B: _____ up straightaway.

4 A: I can't do this exercise. It's too hard.
   B: Don't _____ up. You can do it.

5 A: No one sent me a birthday card!
   B: _____ out your Facebook page!

6 A: Where's your house? I'm in your street.
   B: _____ for a house with a red door. That's ours!

2 Read the message conversation below and complete gaps 1–5 with sentences A–F. There is one extra sentence.

a It even told you what exercise you needed to do.
b I lost it when we were on holiday in Greece.
c You're right – some of those gadgets were brilliant!
d And it was quite heavy and big.
e You can wear it in water.
f It was on at 6.30.

3 Mark the sentences ✓ (right), ✗ (wrong) or ? (doesn't say).

1 ✓ Carrie watched the programme before Marlon.
2 ☐ Marlon agrees with Carrie about the programme.
3 ☐ Marlon liked his watch because it looked good.
4 ☐ Carrie lost her watch too.
5 ☐ Marlon dropped his watch in a swimming pool.

Carrie
Did you see the programme last night about new gadgets? ¹_f_ I watched it with my brother and we both made a list of presents for next year!

Marlon
I got back from football a bit late last night. So I didn't see it at 6.30 but I watched it online later. ²_____ I want the new smartwatch they showed. It's brilliant!

Carrie
But you got a smartwatch last year when you went on holiday to the USA. I remember! You were really proud of it! It gave you lots of interesting information. ³_____ You got emails and everything on it.

Marlon
I know. It was cool. But I didn't like its appearance very much. ⁴_____ Now – this new one … it does everything AND it looks good. I haven't got the American watch anymore. ⁵_____ We went on a boat and it fell it into the water.

Carrie
What a shame!

Marlon
Yes, I was really upset then. But at least now I can ask my parents for a new one for Christmas.

I can make sentences with verbs followed by the to-infinitive or the -ing form.

1 WORD FRIENDS **Match the parts of the sentences.**

1 [b] I sometimes receive
2 [ ] I use my tablet a lot and need to charge
3 [ ] I don't often check
4 [ ] On some trains you can't make
5 [ ] If I'm bored, I play

a the battery every night.
b texts in class but I can't read them then!
c games on my tablet.
d phone calls and that annoys me.
e updates on my smartphone because I'm busy.

2 ● **Complete the table with the verbs below.**

> ~~learn~~ ~~keep~~ don't mind love
> remember prefer decide agree stop
> can't stand try would like enjoy forget
> finish need hate want like

A: Verbs + *to do*	B: Verbs + *ing*
learn	*keep*

3 ●● **Complete the sentences with the correct form of the verbs in brackets.**

1 My mum enjoys *watching* films online. (watch)
2 I prefer _____ to concerts to _____ to the cinema. (go)
3 I sometimes forget _____ my phone overnight. (charge)
4 Jake decided _____ his phone at home for the day! He went crazy! (leave)
5 My gran is learning _____ Facebook – she's doing really well. (use)
6 I can't stand _____ texts on my phone from advertisers. (get)

4 ●●● **Choose the correct option.**

My blog

I love ¹*to go* / *going* on Facebook! Every morning I enjoy ²*to read* / *reading* posts from my friends and ³*to look* / *looking* at the photographs they upload. It's also great for keeping in touch with old friends. If I forget ⁴*to reply* / *replying* to posts or comments, Facebook reminds me! I also like ⁵*to watch* / *watching* video clips, especially funny ones with animals. Last week I decided ⁶*to make* / *making* a video of my cat. I tried ⁷*to film* / *filming* her in my bedroom but she kept ⁸*to run* / *running* out of the room! Then the camera stopped ⁹*to work* / *working*. So I waited until the next day and my brother helped me ¹⁰*to fix* / *fixing* it. It was perfect. I wanted ¹¹*to study* / *studying* film and photography at college but after yesterday – maybe not! I'd also like a job in programming. I learned ¹²*to design* / *designing* websites last year. That was fun!

I can identify specific detail in a conversation and talk about websites.

1 WORD FRIENDS Complete the sentences with the correct verbs.

upload   click   download   share   ~~search~~   chat

1 I often *search* the web for information.
2 I make a lot of videos and I like to _____ them with my friends online.
3 Did you _____ that video of the eagle on the Burj Khalifa from the link I sent you?
4 I often _____ online with my best friend.
5 _____ on the link in this email and you can see the website I told you about.
6 I often _____ photographs to share with my friends on Facebook.

2 🔊 09 Listen to Tom talking to his granddad about a project he did. Complete the notes.

Tom's project is about the history of [1]*computers*.
Tom got an [2]_____ for it.
Tom spent [3]_____ on the project.
Wikipedia began in [4]_____.
There are over five [5]_____ pages of articles.
Tom's granddad wants some information about a favourite [6]_____.

3 🔊 09 Listen again and choose the correct answers.

1 What is Tom's granddad surprised by in Tom's project?
   (a) the age of the first computer
   b Tom's mark
   c how long it took Tom

2 What do 500 million people do every month?
   a write articles for Wikipedia
   b check articles on Wikipedia
   c read articles on Wikipedia

3 Why is Wikipedia popular today?
   a It's quick.
   b It's correct.
   c It's interesting.

4 Where did Tom's granddad get information?
   a in newspapers
   b at school
   c at the library

5 People check articles now to be sure that
   a they're correct.
   b they're interesting.
   c they're well-written.

4 🔊 10 Complete the sentences from the dialogue with the correct prepositions. Then listen and check.

1 Did you spend a long time *on* it?
2 I spent an hour looking for the information and then another two hours typing it _____.
3 You can look _____ anything!
4 You just type _____ the subject and it's all there in front of you.
5 Can I go on this site to find _____ about a writer that I like?

5 Choose the correct option.

1 I'd like to find *on* /(*out*) about some new apps for my tablet.
2 I spent three hours *for / on* my homework last night.
3 Where do I type *on / in* the name of the site?
4 Can you look *up / down* this word in the dictionary please?
5 Here are my notes for the essay. Now I'm going to type them *off / up*.

I can put events in order when talking about the past.

1 WORD FRIENDS **Complete the sentences with the correct words.**

give   crashed   ~~connect~~   program
working   died   virus   up

1 I can't **connect** a microphone to my PC. Could you _____ me a hand?
2 A: Hi – what's _____?
   B: My computer _____ yesterday and I can't get online.
3 Do you fancy coming over to help me with my computer? It's got a _____!
4 Sorry I couldn't phone earlier. The battery in my phone _____.
5 Help! My internet connection stopped _____ this morning! Can I come to your house and use your computer?
6 I tried to download the _____ last night but I think it was too big. Did you manage to download it?

2 **Complete the sentences with the correct words.**

suddenly   end   that   Finally
~~first~~   later   then   all

1 My phone rang. At *first*, there was silence. _____ my uncle said, 'Hi Brian!'
2 I switched on my hair dryer. First of _____ there was a strange noise. A few moments _____ it stopped working.
3 I was on my computer when _____ I smelled burning!
4 I spent hours on my essay last night. _____ I finished it at midnight.
5 Just before class I called my mum on the phone. After _____ I switched it off.
6 I tried to fix the problem on my laptop but in the _____ I asked my clever friend Dave to help!

3 **Put the events in the correct order. Then add the time words to the beginning of the sentences.**

A ~~At first~~ / Then / Finally
   a ☐ *At first*, I really enjoyed checking posts.
   b ☐ 1 I started using Facebook a year ago.
   c ☐ _____ I stopped using it completely and started using Twitter.
   d ☐ _____ I got a bit bored.

B First of all / Next / In the end
   a ☐ _____ we had to tell the class our answers.
   b ☐ We had an interesting computer lesson today.
   c ☐ _____ she put us in small groups to compare our answers.
   d ☐ _____ the teacher gave us a questionnaire to fill in.

C First / After that / Finally
   a ☐ _____ we learned to write simple programs.
   b ☐ _____ we took a test and we all passed.
   c ☐ _____ we did more difficult things.
   d ☐ I started learning to code when I was ten.

4 🔊 11 **Match gaps 1–6 with sentences a–f. Then listen and check.**

A: Hiya, Karen! It's good to SEE you!
B: Yeah – I finally got my laptop with webcam!
A: When did you get it?
B: ¹d But it was very old and it was impossible. I needed a new one.
A: Very true!
B: ²___
A: Yeah – they aren't cheap.
B: So dad went to talk to mum. ³___
A: Your parents are cool!
B: Yeah, I think so. ⁴___
A: Did you choose a really expensive one?
B: No, I didn't! At first, I didn't know which one to get. There were lots! ⁵___ There was one laptop for three hundred pounds and another for two hundred!
A: Those are very good prices!
B: So, we thought about it. ⁶___ It's great!

a After that they took me to the computer shop to buy one!
b Then I saw some special offers.
c But I didn't have enough money.
d Well, first I asked my dad to fix my old laptop.
e In the end we decided to get the £300 one.
f So we looked round the shop.

I can be specific about people, things and places.

1 Match the parts of the sentences.

1　[b]　That's the teacher
2　☐　That's the picture
3　☐　That's the town
4　☐　That's a photo of the singer
5　☐　That's the book
6　☐　That's the actress

a　that I borrowed from Lara.
b　who taught me Maths in Year 10.
c　where we went on holiday last summer.
d　who recorded the song *My Time*.
e　that I painted.
f　who was really good in the film *The Maze Runner*.

2 Use the clues to complete the crossword.

Across

2　It's a group of online pages that are about the same topic.
3　It's something that we download regularly to make computers and phones work better.
6　It's any new electronic machine which is new and useful.
8　It's a type of traditional computer which is fixed in one place and we don't carry around.

Down

1　It's something bad that can hurt a computer.
4　It's something that we send to a friend on a phone.
5　It's something that we use to move round the screen.
7　It's a programme we download on a smartphone which has a specific purpose.

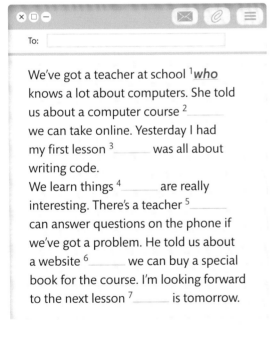

3 Complete the email with the correct words.

To:

We've got a teacher at school ¹**who** knows a lot about computers. She told us about a computer course ² _____ we can take online. Yesterday I had my first lesson ³ _____ was all about writing code.
We learn things ⁴ _____ are really interesting. There's a teacher ⁵ _____ can answer questions on the phone if we've got a problem. He told us about a website ⁶ _____ we can buy a special book for the course. I'm looking forward to the next lesson ⁷ _____ is tomorrow.

For each learning objective, tick (✓) the box that best matches your ability.

😊😊 = I understand and can help a friend.   ☹ = I understand but have some questions.

😊 = I understand and can do it by myself.   ☹☹ = I do not understand.

		😊😊	😊	☹	☹☹	Need help?	Now try ...
4.1	Vocabulary					Students' Book pp. 46–47 Workbook pp. 42–43	Ex. 1–3, p. 51
4.2	Grammar					Students' Book p. 48 Workbook p. 44	Ex. 4–6, p. 51
4.3	Reading					Students' Book p. 49 Workbook p. 45	
4.4	Grammar					Students' Book p. 50 Workbook p. 46	
4.5	Listening					Students' Book p. 51 Workbook p. 47	
4.6	Speaking					Students' Book p. 52 Workbook p. 48	Ex. 7, p. 51
4.7	English in Use					Students' Book p. 53 Workbook p. 49	

4.1   I can talk about technology.
4.2   I can use the Past Simple of irregular verbs to talk about the past.
4.3   I can find specific detail in a text and talk about using technology.
4.4   I can make sentences with verbs followed by the infinitive or the gerund.
4.5   I can identify specific detail in a conversation and talk about websites.
4.6   I can put events in order when talking about the past.
4.7   I can be specific about people, things and places.

What can you remember from this unit?

New words I learned (the words you most want to remember from this unit)	**Expressions and phrases I liked** (any expressions or phrases you think sound nice, useful or funny)	**English I heard or read outside class** (e.g. from websites, books, adverts, films, music)

Vocabulary

1 Complete the words from the descriptions.

1 We play computer games on this:
   c _ _ _ _ _ _ _

2 Your phone works when you put this in it: **b** _ _ _ _ _ _ _

3 You can copy files onto this:
   p _ _ **d** _ _ _ _ _

4 You type on this: **k** _ _ _ _ _ _ _ _

5 You take photos with this:
   d _ _ _ _ _ _ _ **c** _ _ _ _ _ _

6 You can carry this small computer easily: **t** _ _ _ _ _ _

2 Complete the sentences with the correct words.

| chat   charge   check   click |
| make   text |

1 I _____ my emails every hour.

2 My friend and I _____ online after school.

3 I sometimes _____ my friends during lessons!

4 You need to _____ your phone battery every night.

5 We often _____ video clips and put them online.

6 You must _____ on this link to get to the website.

3 Choose the correct option.

1 Can you help me *put / connect* a microphone?

2 My computer *fell / crashed* yesterday so I didn't do any work.

3 The battery in my camera *died / emptied* and I couldn't take any photos.

4 Our internet connection *stopped / finished* working and I had to wait hours!

5 I didn't have enough memory to *remember / download* the software.

6 Don't open that email or you might get a(n) *illness / virus*.

Grammar

4 Complete the sentences with the correct past form of the verbs in brackets.

1 I _____ to do my homework last night. (forget)

2 I _____ my book on the bus this morning. (leave)

3 The teacher _____ us a lot of work in class today. (not give)

4 _____ the computer _____ a lot of money? (cost)

5 My brother _____ the dog for a walk early today. (take)

6 Someone _____ my dad's car last week. (steal)

5 Complete the sentences with the correct form of the verbs.

| feed   go   help   learn   watch   work |

1 I enjoyed _____ the film with you yesterday.

2 What time did you stop _____ on the computer last night?

3 I agreed _____ to the party with Ben.

4 I don't mind _____ you with your homework.

5 Jason decided _____ to drive next year.

6 Don't forget _____ the cat this evening.

6 Complete the sentences with *who, which* or *where*.

1 The person _____ helped me with the project was Ruth.

2 The place _____ we first met was the library.

3 That's the book _____ you gave me for my birthday.

4 That's the office _____ my dad works.

5 This is the restaurant _____ Ronnie recommended.

6 That's the teacher _____ first taught me English.

Speaking language practice

7 Complete the text with the correct words.

| after   ago   all   At   end   later |

Two days ¹_____ we went to a computer shop to buy a laptop. First of ²_____ we looked at a very new one. ³_____ first, we couldn't see the price but then we saw it on the shelf. It was very expensive! We looked at a couple of other ones and ⁴_____ that we went for a coffee to think about it. Half an hour ⁵_____ we went back and looked at some more. In the ⁶_____ we decided to buy the first one! It's amazing!

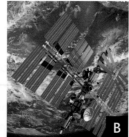

1 Match words and phrases 1–7 with the photos A–G.

1 [F] a cab
2 [ ] an ice camp
3 [ ] a selfie
4 [ ] an engineer
5 [ ] a route
6 [ ] a satellite
7 [ ] a summit

2 Choose the correct option.

1 They (set) / made up a hotspot at the top of a mountain.
2 I looked / browsed the internet last night for an hour.
3 We did / made the journey from the north to the south of Europe.
4 I opened / went online this morning to check my emails.

3 Complete the sentences with the correct words.

connection countryside free receiver ~~remote~~

1 My friend teaches English in a _remote_ area of Africa.
2 If you want to get the internet, there must be a _____ near you.
3 Jo lives in the _____ but she'd like to live in the town.
4 My smartphone came with a lot of _____ apps.
5 We don't have a very good internet _____ where I live.

4 Complete the words in the sentences.

1 A company that is big and strong is **powerful**.
2 The _ _ v _ _ n _ _ _ _ t makes decisions about what will happen in a country.
3 The things that companies make and sell are called _ r _ d _ _ t _ .
4 We need _ q _ i _ _ _ n _ to do certain jobs, sports or activities.
5 You are _ _ o _ if you don't have a lot of money.

5 Complete the sentences with the correct verbs.

benefit compete earn give grow
~~make~~ sell spy

1 Computers _make_ a big difference to students' education.
2 The police _____ on people they think are criminals.
3 Farmers _____ crops in their fields.
4 I have a new computer. I want to _____ my old one away.
5 You look tired. You might _____ from a break.
6 How much money did you _____ last month?
7 We _____ with another school at sport every weekend.
8 These shops _____ products that are environmentally-friendly.

6 Make sentences in the Past Simple.

1 Tim Berners-Lee / create / something amazing
    Tim Berners-Lee created something amazing.
2 Kudjo / sell / his crops / for a lot of money
    _____
3 the internet / change / people's lives / when / it / start
    _____
4 Tim Berners-Lee / invent / the internet
    _____
5 he / not know / his invention was so important
    _____
6 the boys / come / from a nearby village
    _____

7 Read the video script. Underline any words or phrases you don't know and find their meaning in your dictionary.

The digital revolution
Part 1

This is Africa. It's a beautiful place. The first human beings came from Africa. But today we're here to think about the future, not the past. Today, something important is happening in a small town in Ghana. It is plugging into the
5 internet. There are still a lot of countries in Africa that do not have internet connection. But this is changing, slowly. The internet makes a big difference to people's lives and nearly everything they do. Today, that difference is starting here. And the people have a special visitor on this special day, Sir Tim Berners-Lee. Tim is an important man and people admire him a lot.
10 More than twenty years ago he invented the World Wide Web. He wanted to connect people all over the world. He had a wonderful idea.
He wanted everyone, rich and poor, to use it. Money wasn't important for him. He thought it should be free for everyone. Then people could learn lots of information and share their ideas. Now these people in Ghana can do that.
15 Tim is showing these African people how to use electronic equipment to search the web. They see the things they can learn and how they can keep in touch with other people.
But what does the internet really mean for the people here in Africa and for everyone who is connected? Is the internet good for us, or bad?

20 ## Part 2

The world today is very different because of the web. Now there are three billion people online. The internet gives us information, friends and a lot more. Life is easier. We can go online nearly everywhere – at home, outside and in cafés. And many people are now very rich because of the internet. Very big
25 companies like Google, Amazon and eBay earn billions of pounds.
But some people think there are bad things about the web. Is it a good thing for these companies to be so big and powerful? Should governments use the internet to spy on people? Can we stop people becoming addicted to computer games? There are some big problems. But Tim Berners-Lee's idea
30 – to connect people who are not rich or powerful – is still true. Kudjo is a successful farmer in Ghana and for him the internet is very important.
At first, he didn't know how to use the web. Then a friend gave him some practical lessons. Now he browses for information. The internet helps him to grow his crops and to sell them. He checks out the prices of different
35 products. Then he can sell his products at the correct price. He can compete with the big farmers now and he can earn more money. Kudjo feels connected to the world, not alone.
This is what Tim Berners-Lee wanted when he invented the web. He created something amazing and it's still changing today. But he never earned money
40 from it. He gave it away to the world for free because he wanted everyone to benefit from it. These young people in Africa today are doing exactly that. What a wonderful present!

I can talk about things in the house.

My home, my town

1 ● **Choose the odd one out.**

1 cooker   sink   (bookcase)   tap
2 armchair   toilet   rug   coffee table
3 chair   bed   washing machine   wardrobe
4 shower   bath   washbasin   sofa
5 wall   switch   floor   ceiling
6 bedroom   bathroom   mirror   kitchen

2 ● **Find eight words from Exercise 1 in the word search.**

S	S	S	M	Y	W	C	G	O	B
W	M	H	D	S	A	U	M	E	E
I	I	K	R	A	S	P	T	A	P
T	R	S	M	R	H	B	T	O	X
C	R	A	O	M	B	O	X	M	T
H	O	V	I	C	A	A	K	K	O
R	R	U	X	H	S	R	F	L	I
D	D	L	V	A	I	D	L	P	L
N	K	B	G	I	N	A	Q	N	E
P	N	F	A	R	W	V	B	N	T

3 ●● **Complete the sentences with the correct words.**

curtains   tap   mirror   floor   ~~wardrobe~~   lamp

1 I need a new *wardrobe* to put all my clothes in.
2 I often switch on the _____ by my bed and read before I go to sleep.
3 I looked in the _____ and saw that my hair was a mess.
4 Can I have different coloured _____ in my bedroom? These striped ones are old!
5 The _____ in the bathroom isn't working. I can't get any water.
6 When I walk on my bedroom _____ it makes a noise!

4 ●● **Complete the words from the descriptions.**

1 You wash yourself in here: **s**hower
2 You put dirty clothes in this: **w** _ _ _ _ _ _ _   **m** _ _ _ _ _ _ _
3 You turn this to get water: **t** _ _
4 You put books in this: **b** _ _ _ _ _ _ _
5 You keep packets of food in this: **c** _ _ _ _ _ _ _
6 You look in this to see your face: **m** _ _ _ _ _
7 You have these at your window: **c** _ _ _ _ _ _ _
8 This gives you light: **l** _ _ _ _

5 ● Look at the picture and complete the sentences with the correct words or phrases.

> under   in front of   opposite   next to
> behind   above   ~~on~~   between

1 The cat is lying *on* the rug.
2 The dog is _____ to the cat.
3 They are _____ the fire.
4 The fire is _____ the two bookcases.
5 A clock is _____ the fire.
6 A letter is _____ the clock.
7 My school bag is _____ the table.
8 The table is _____ the sofa.

6 ●● Choose the correct answers.

1 Are those your dirty plates in the _____?
   a desk   ⓑ sink   c cupboard
2 I left my book on the _____.
   a tap   b bedside table   c mirror
3 I want to buy a new _____ for the bedroom floor.
   a lamp   b bed   c rug
4 Come here and sit _____ me on the sofa.
   a next to   b between   c above
5 I sat _____ Tim at dinner.
   a opposite   b above   c between

7 ●● Use the letters to write the correct words.

1 Sorry I was in the WHORSE *shower* and I didn't hear the phone.
2 Leave the bath and the SHAWIBANS _____ clean, please!
3 The light TWISHC _____ in my bedroom isn't working.
4 Granddad is in his CRAMIRHA _____. He's watching TV.
5 Don't walk on the ROLFO _____ with your dirty boots! It's clean.
6 I like a dark bedroom at night so I always close my SCANTIUR _____.
7 When I lie on my bed and look at the NIICELG, _____ I can see a strange mark.
8 My essay was on my KEDS _____ but it isn't there now.

8 ●●● Complete the email with the correct words.

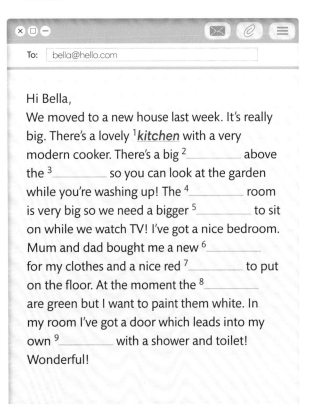

To: bella@hello.com

Hi Bella,
We moved to a new house last week. It's really big. There's a lovely [1]*kitchen* with a very modern cooker. There's a big [2]_____ above the [3]_____ so you can look at the garden while you're washing up! The [4]_____ room is very big so we need a bigger [5]_____ to sit on while we watch TV! I've got a nice bedroom. Mum and dad bought me a new [6]_____ for my clothes and a nice red [7]_____ to put on the floor. At the moment the [8]_____ are green but I want to paint them white. In my room I've got a door which leads into my own [9]_____ with a shower and toilet! Wonderful!

1 **WORD FRIENDS** Complete the sentences with the correct verbs.

> set ~~do~~ make dry load sweep take tidy

1 Mum and dad <u>do</u> the shopping every Saturday morning.
2 Can you _____ the dishwasher while I _____ the rubbish out?
3 My brother didn't _____ his bed this morning and his room's a mess.
4 We have to _____ the floor every day because of our dog's hairs!
5 I usually _____ my room at the weekend.
6 I can wash the dishes if you _____ them.
7 I need to _____ the table for five people.

2 Choose the correct option.

1 I usually eat my breakfast very quick /(quickly).
2 My young sister is a very happy / happily little girl.
3 Jack waved to me cheerful / cheerfully when I saw him this morning.
4 The man shouted at the dog angry / angrily.
5 The students chatted noisy / noisily while they waited for the teacher.
6 Paul is a really bad / badly tennis player and no one wants to play with him!

3 Make adverbs from the adjectives. Then complete the table with the adverbs.

> ~~fast~~ ~~careful~~ angry late bad hard
> slow cheerful early right noisy sad
> wrong quick

A	Adjectives that take –ly ending for adverbs: *carefully*
B	Adjectives that stay the same when adverbs: *fast*

4 Complete the sentences with the correct adverbs.

1 She's a slow driver. She drives <u>slowly</u>.
2 He's a fast learner. He learns _____.
3 I'm a careful writer. I write _____.
4 My dad's a hard worker. He works _____.
5 He's a good footballer. He plays football _____.
6 I gave the wrong answer. I got the answer _____.
7 I was late for the meeting. I arrived _____.
8 My sister's a bad cook. She cooks _____.

5 Match the parts of the sentences.

1 [c] Jack spoke so quietly that
2 [ ] The party was so noisy that
3 [ ] Mike drove so fast that
4 [ ] Tom's results were so good that
5 [ ] Dave ran so slowly that
6 [ ] My dad got up so early that

a Leo's neighbour complained.
b he was last in the race.
c the teacher didn't hear him.
d he was tired by lunchtime.
e he arrived very early.
f his parents gave him a present.

6 Choose the correct option.

● ● ● My page

I had a really ¹(bad)/ badly day yesterday. First I got up ²late / lately and I didn't have time for a shower. Then I ate my breakfast ³so / very quickly and I felt ill on the bus to school! I forgot to ⁴take / make the rubbish out and my dad was ⁵angry / angrily. In Maths I got all the test questions ⁶wrong / wrongly and the teacher gave me extra work. I tried to do my History homework in the evening but my computer was ⁷so / very slow that I gave up. It was my turn to ⁸tidy / clear the living room but I didn't vacuum it ⁹careful / carefully and my mum told me to do it again. Then something went ¹⁰right / rightly! I watched a ¹¹late / lately football match on TV. My favourite team played very ¹²good / well and they won. But I shouted so noisily ¹³than / that my mum sent me to my room. Oh well …

1 Complete the sentences with the correct adjectives.

> messy large narrow ~~bright~~
> cosy modern

1 My bedroom is quite dark but your room is lovely and *bright*.
2 The sofa in our last house was big and uncomfortable but this one is nice and _____.
3 The hotel had wide corridors downstairs but upstairs they were very _____.
4 This wardrobe is too small for all my dresses and I need a _____ one.
5 My mum likes old-fashioned furniture but my dad prefers _____ things.
6 These days my room is always tidy but when I was younger it was very _____.

2 Read the story. Mark the sentences ✓ (right), ✗ (wrong) or ? (doesn't say).

1 ✗ The girl listened to a story on her headphones.
2 ☐ The girl did the same things every night.
3 ☐ She heard a man's voice.
4 ☐ It got cold in her room.
5 ☐ The girl has two sisters.
6 ☐ The house shook when the tree fell.
7 ☐ The tree fell because it was old.

3 Complete the sentences with the correct prepositions.

> out up at down ~~on~~ out of

1 I switched *on* my lamp and read my book.
2 I pulled _____ my headphones to listen to my friend.
3 I jumped _____ bed when I heard the noise.
4 I ran _____ the road to try to catch the bus.
5 My dad pointed _____ the tree. There was a bird's nest at the top of it.

An **important** message

It was quite late and I was in bed. Outside it was very dark and the weather was bad. The wind was loud in the trees. But my bedroom was warm and cosy. I put my headphones on to listen to my favourite music and started to read my book. I always listened to music and read before I went to sleep.

Suddenly the music stopped. I looked at my MP3 player. It was still switched on. Then a voice spoke quietly in my headphones. 'Get out of your bedroom. Now.' I felt a bit frightened. Who was it? I looked round. I was alone. My door was closed, the window was closed … everyone was asleep, the house was quiet.

Then the voice spoke again. 'Get out. Now!' I was so scared that I dropped my book on the floor. Suddenly my room didn't feel warm and cosy. It felt scary. There were lots of dark places outside the circle of light from my bedside lamp.

'Now!' this time the voice shouted loudly. I pulled out my headphones quickly and jumped out of bed. I ran to the door and opened it. Behind me there was a very loud noise. I didn't look back. I ran down the corridor and down the stairs.

Then there was another very loud noise from upstairs and the cupboards in the hall moved. My mum and sisters ran down the stairs too. 'What's happening?' I screamed. My dad came down and pushed us all outside into the garden.

'Look,' he said and pointed up at my room. A large tree was on the roof. Part of it was in my room. The windows were broken. I don't know who it was but the voice in my headphones saved my life that night.

I can talk about permission and obligation.

1 ● Complete the sentences with *can* or *can't*.

1 I *can't* come round to see you tonight because my mum wants me to tidy my room.

2 We _____ use smartphones in class – not even to go online and look for information!

3 You _____ borrow my tablet if you want.

4 _____ we look in the dictionary during the test?

5 I _____ learn to drive now because I'm too young.

6 My brother _____ watch TV until 11, but I _____ . That's not fair!

2 ● Order the words to make sentences or questions.

1 leave / have / soon / you / to / do / ?
Do you have to leave soon?

2 has / my / early / get / to / up / dad
_____
_____

3 to / room / don't / tidy / have / my / I
_____
_____
_____

4 your / day / cook / does / have / mum / to / every / ?
_____
_____
_____

5 doesn't / outside / my / sleep / have / dog / to
_____
_____
_____

6 housework / have / the / you / help / to / with / do / ?
_____
_____

3 ● Make sentences or questions with the correct form of *have to*.

1 you / get home / before 10.30 / ?
Do you have to get home before 10.30?

2 we / not / do / Exercise 4 / for homework
_____

3 the teacher / arrive / at school / before 8.00
_____

4 Peter / not / take the rubbish out / at weekends
_____

5 your dad / take / the train to work / ?
_____

6 at university / my sister / not / get up early every day
_____

4 ● Choose the correct answers.

1 We _____ give in this work before Thursday. We've got three days!
   a mustn't   ⓑ don't have to   c can't

2 You _____ shout at your brother. He didn't do anything.
   a mustn't   b don't have to   c can't

3 I _____ go on that website because I haven't got a password.
   a mustn't   b don't have to   c can't

4 You _____ join the photography club because it's full.
   a mustn't   b don't have to   c can't

5 Olly _____ work at the supermarket next weekend. It's a holiday.
   a mustn't   b doesn't have to   c can't

6 You _____ touch that key. It deletes everything!
   a mustn't   b don't have to   c can

5 ●●● Complete the dialogue with one word in each gap.

A: Hi! Do you have ¹ *to* work this weekend?

B: No, I ² _____ . I haven't got any work so I ³ _____ do what I want! Why?

A: It's my birthday and I ⁴ _____ invite two friends to stay! Would you like to come?

B: Cool! Yes, please.

A: Can your sister Elise come too?

B: No, I'm afraid she ⁵ _____ . She was late home last week and now she ⁶ _____ to stay home and help with the housework!

A: That's a shame. How long ⁷ _____ she have to do that for?

B: Only for a week. Anyway – I ⁸ _____ to go now. I ⁹ _____ get to my next lesson.

I can identify specific detail in a conversation and talk about my town.

1 Look at photos 1–6 and complete the words in the crossword. What is number 6?

	6		
¹p	a	r	k
	2		
3			
	4		
5			

2 Complete the words from the descriptions.

1 You go here to watch a film:
c*inema*

2 This is a place where a lot of people live in similar houses:
e _ _ _ _ _ _

3 People go here on Sundays:
c _ _ _ _ _

4 You can look at old things here:
m _ _ _ _ _

5 You go here to send letters:
p _ _ _ o _ _ _ _ _

3 🔊 12 Listen to a conversation between James and Alice. Complete gaps 1–5 with a word or phrase.

PAXFORD

TOURIST INFORMATION CENTRE

Popular place to visit:	The ¹*Mann* Art Gallery
Started in:	² _____
Location:	in the ³ _____ next to the station.
Ticket prices:	Adults: £10.50
	Students: ⁴ _____
Opening times:	9.30 am – ⁵ _____ pm

4 🔊 12 Listen again. Tick the things Alice says there are at the art gallery.

1 ☑ a café
2 ☐ nice gardens
3 ☐ some statues
4 ☐ some Percy Mann paintings
5 ☐ pictures of Paxford town
6 ☐ a poster exhibition
7 ☐ a picture of a castle
8 ☐ some paintings of the sea
9 ☐ a gift shop

I can ask for, give and receive advice.

1 Complete the sentences with the correct words.

| should think thanks terrible
| ~~advice~~ don't good why

1 Can you give me some _advice_ about the best smartphones to buy at the moment?

2 That's a _____ idea. _____ for the advice.

3 _____ don't you talk to your teacher about your problems?

4 Where _____ I go to buy some new trainers?

5 I _____ think you should try to fix your computer yourself.

6 What do you _____ I should wear to the party?

7 That's a _____ idea! I can't do that!

2 Choose the correct answers.

1 Where should I go on holiday?
   a I don't think that's a good idea.
   b Thanks for the advice.
   c Why don't you go to France?

2 You shouldn't work so hard.
   a That's a terrible idea.
   b Thanks for the advice.
   c It's not your fault.

3 Can you give me some advice about my room?
   a I think you should get some new posters.
   b That's a good idea.
   c What should I do?

4 Why don't you have a break?
   a I think you should relax.
   b That's a good idea.
   c Good for you!

3 Order the sentences to make conversations.

1 a ☐ Why don't you try the new shop in the shopping mall?
   b ☐ That's a good idea. Thanks.
   c ☐1 I need to get a new smartphone. Where should I go to get one?

2 a ☐ That's a terrible idea! She hates books!
   b ☐ You should get her a new book. I often buy books for presents.
   c ☐ It's my sister's birthday tomorrow. What do you think I should get her?

3 a ☐ I think you should go to the National Gallery. It's brilliant!
   b ☐ Can you give me some advice about where to go in London?
   c ☐ Thanks for the advice. I like art galleries.

4 🔊 13 Match gaps 1–7 with sentences a–g. Then listen and check.

A: Hi! Good to see you! How's the new school?
B: It's OK. I started last week. The lessons are fine but I don't know ANYONE. ¹_d_
A: It's always hard when you start a new school. ²__ You can meet people who have the same hobbies as you.
B: ³__ There's an art club and a singing club. I can try those.
A: ⁴__ Everyone likes people who have parties!
B: Mm … ⁵__ Our house is very small. And dad is still working on it. He's got to do a lot more painting and building.
A: Maybe your new friends can help!
B: But first I have to find some new friends!
A: ⁶__ You can ask them about where to go in town. People like giving advice!
B: Excellent idea! ⁷__
A: No problem.

a Thanks for the advice! I feel better now.
b That's a good idea.
c I know – why don't you ask a couple of classmates to go shopping with you?
d What do you think I should do to meet people and make friends?
e And why don't you have a party at your new house?
f I think you should join an after school club.
g I don't think that's a good idea.

I can write a personal email.

1 Complete the email with the correct words.

> called   in x2   guess   far   ~~you~~   care
> on   have   flat   well

To: claire@emails.com

Hi Claire,

A

How are ¹*you*? I hope you're ² _____ and that you passed all your exams! I'm fine. ³ _____ what! I'm in France! I'm staying with my French friend Jacques for a week and it's amazing.

B

He lives in a small village. It's ⁴ _____ Beauchamp. It's ⁵ _____ the north of France and it's not ⁶ _____ from the sea. There aren't many houses or shops but there's a baker's and a small supermarket. There isn't a railway station but you can catch a bus to the next town.

C

Jacques lives with his family in a lovely ⁷ _____. It's ⁸ _____ the third floor. It's in a very old house but everything inside is modern. I really like the high ceilings and big windows. It's ⁹ _____ a very quiet area. From his bedroom window you can see across the countryside. It's really beautiful.

D

I ¹⁰ _____ to go now because Jacques' mum is calling me for dinner. The food here is wonderful! Take ¹¹ _____!
Ryan

2 Read the email again. Match paragraphs A–D with the information 1–5. One paragraph gives two pieces of information.

1 [C] a description of Jacques' home
2 [ ] some news in Ryan's life
3 [ ] a reason for finishing the email
4 [ ] a comment about Claire's life
5 [ ] a description of Jacques' town

3 Match the pairs of sentences. Then join the sentences with *and*, *but*, *because* or *so*.

a [5] We went to the beach.
b [ ] I bought some postcards.
c [ ] We spoke English a lot.
d [ ] I didn't like the cheese.
e [ ] Jacques took me to an art gallery.

1 I forgot to send them.
2 I didn't try it again!
3 It wasn't open on Wednesdays.
4 Jacques needs to improve.
5 We swam in the sea.

a *We went to the beach and we swam in the sea.*
b _____
c _____
d _____
e _____

4 Imagine you stayed with a friend in another town or village. Write an email to tell your friend about the town.

a Use the text in Exercise 1 as a model.
b Divide the email into four paragraphs:
   1 Ask for and give news
   2 Describe the place
   3 Describe the house
   4 Close the email
c Remember to begin and end the email with appropriate phrases.
d Connect your ideas with linking words.

☺☺ = I understand and can help a friend.   ☹ = I understand but have some questions.

☺ – I understand and can do it by myself.   ☹☹ = I do not understand.

		☺☺	☺	☹	☹☹	Need help?	Now try ...
5.1	Vocabulary					Students' Book pp. 58–59 Workbook pp. 54–55	Ex. 1–3, p. 63
5.2	Grammar					Students' Book p. 60 Workbook p. 56	Ex. 4–5, p. 63
5.3	Reading					Students' Book p. 61 Workbook p. 57	
5.4	Grammar					Students' Book p. 62 Workbook p. 58	
5.5	Listening					Students' Book p. 63 Workbook p. 59	
5.6	Speaking					Students' Book p. 64 Workbook p. 60	Ex. 6, p. 63
5.7	Writing					Students' Book p. 65 Workbook p. 61	

5.1   I can talk about things in the house.
5.2   I can describe how people do things.
5.3   I can find specific detail in a text and describe places.
5.4   I can talk about permission and obligation.
5.5   I can identify specific detail in a conversation and talk about my town.
5.6   I can ask for, give and receive advice.
5.7   I can write a personal email.

What can you remember from this unit?

New words I learned (the words you most want to remember from this unit)	**Expressions and phrases I liked** (any expressions or phrases you think sound nice, useful or funny)	**English I heard or read outside class** (e.g. from websites, books, adverts, films, music)

1 Choose the correct answers.

1 I put a new poster on my bedroom _____ .
   a window   b wall   c switch
2 My dad always sits in the same _____ .
   a bookcase b coffee table c armchair
3 The cat usually sleeps _____ the table.
   a over   b between   c under
4 I need a _____ for my bedroom floor.
   a rug   b cupboard   c sink
5 Do you like our _____ new curtains?
   a tidy   b comfortable c bright
6 I can't get any water from this _____ .
   a tap   b lamp   c cooker

2 Choose the correct option.

1 I didn't *take / make* my bed this morning.
2 On Saturdays I *sweep / tidy* the floor to help my mum.
3 We usually *do / make* the shopping on Friday evenings.
4 Can you *sweep / empty* the dishwasher, please?
5 My sister never *washes / tidies* her room.
6 Dad *made / took* the rubbish out after dinner.

3 Complete the words in the sentences.

1 Our class went to the art **g**_____ last week.
2 My friend works at the police **s**_____ .
3 The new shopping **c**_____ in town is brilliant.
4 There's a big meeting at the town **h**_____ about the new estate.
5 I must go to the post **o**_____ to send these letters.
6 Why don't we get some brochures from the Tourist **I**_____ **C**_____ ?

4 Complete the sentences with adverbs from the adjectives in brackets.

1 I worked really _____ to pass this test. (hard)
2 My dad shouted _____ at the cat when it scratched the table. (angry)
3 Hester ran _____ and won the race. (good)
4 The little girl wrote her name _____ at the top of the drawing. (careful)
5 The computer downloaded the file very _____ . (quick)
6 We all arrived _____ and we had to wait. (early)

5 Complete the sentences with the correct form of *can*, *must* or *have to*.

1 We _____ finish this work before Friday. That's great!
2 The teacher says we _____ leave early today because we worked really hard this morning.
3 You _____ touch that dog. It's dangerous.
4 I _____ get on that website because I haven't got a password.
5 My dad _____ work on Saturdays so we do the shopping on Sundays.
6 I _____ be late again! The teacher was very angry with me today.

6 Order the words to make questions or sentences in the dialogue.

A: ¹some / you / advice / give / can / me / ?
   _____

B: Sure. What's the problem?
A: I'm going to London with my friend.
   ²think / where / go / you / should / we / do / ? _____
B: ³should / to / think / I / you / go / the British Museum _____ It's great.
A: ⁴that's / don't / a / idea / think / good / I _____ My friend hates museums!
B: OK! ⁵don't / to / you / gallery / why / art / go / an / ? _____
A: ⁶for / thanks / advice / the _____
   ⁷great / that's / idea / a _____

1 Match words 1–5 with photos A–E.

1 E bricks   3 ☐ block   5 ☐ wood
2 ☐ stilts   4 ☐ shapes

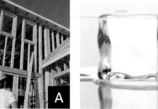

2 Complete the sentences with the correct form of the words from Exercise 1.

1 The boy looked really tall because he was walking on _stilts_!
2 People cut down trees to get _____ to build houses.
3 The children painted different _____.
4 People in Greenland build their houses out of _____ of ice!
5 They are building the house out of _____.

3 Label photos 1–8 with the correct words.

| alcove blind doorstops glass case sewing machine
shelves ~~wallpaper~~ work station |

wallpaper _____ _____

4 What can you remember about the unit video? Mark the sentences T (true) or F (false).

1 T Hattie and Freya **share** a room.
2 ☐ Their mum **designs** their new room.
3 ☐ Michelle **surprises** the girls with some new furniture.
4 ☐ They **stick** photographs of their cats on the wallpaper.
5 ☐ Their mum **throws** everything from the front room away.

5 Complete the sentences with the correct form of the verbs in bold from Exercise 4.

1 My sister _sticks_ notes on her desk so that she doesn't forget things!
2 I would like to _____ clothes and accessories when I'm older.
3 At lunchtime, my friend and I often _____ our sandwiches.
4 I have a lot of old clothes that I must _____ away – I don't need them.
5 Mum wants to _____ dad by getting him a laptop for his birthday.

6 Use the clues to complete the crossword. What's the mystery word?

1 These walls are made of something very hard and strong.
2 This person doesn't work in daylight. He works underground.
3 We burn this on the fire to keep warm.
4 You might find this in a front room, beside the fireplace.
5 A big, thick piece of wood or ice.
6 We use this to keep the door open.
7 When you stand on these, you're very tall!
8 Put this over the window instead of curtains.
9 This person hates you and wants to hurt you.

Mystery word: _____

	¹B	R	I	C	K		
2							
			3				
4							
5							
			6				
7							
	8						
9							

7 Read the video script. Underline any words or phrases you don't know and find their meaning in your dictionary.

I want my own room!

Part 1

What's your room like? What would you like to change about it? Would you like to design it yourself? The programme *I want my own room!* helps kids change their rooms. Today they're helping Freya and her younger
5 sister, Hattie.
Both girls love to make things. Freya likes sewing and Hattie likes making films – she wants to be a film director. Their older sister Ella has her own room and their mum makes plates and paints them. She has lots of space. Even the cats, Lola and Rose, have room to relax. Hattie and Freya share a
10 nice room but they need more space for their hobbies. It's a big problem! There is one room that they can use. It's the front room, and it's the girls' playroom. The problem is … it's full of rubbish! There are old toys and a doll's house. But it isn't all the girls' rubbish – there's even a bit of an old car in there! Michelle is an artist and designer. She's going to help the girls to
15 make their dream room.

Part 2

Michelle talks to the girls about how to change the room. They paint a plan on the wall. Michelle thinks each girl can have one of the alcoves in the room for their things.
20 Mum has to clear the front room but she can't do it on her own, so big sister Ella comes to help. Now they must choose what to throw away and what to keep. It isn't easy!
The girls make a floor plan for the room. Michelle thinks there can be a sofa and work stations for the girls, so they can do their different hobbies.
25 She also suggests special wallpaper. The girls choose old photographs from when they were younger to stick on to it.

Part 3

Everyone works hard to finish the room in four days. Michelle keeps the last changes a secret. She wants to surprise Freya and Hattie. They paint
30 butterflies on the walls and the shelves are a lovely colour too. There's a fun, home-made doorstop to keep the door open and there are some fantastic cushions. They have photographs of the family cats on them. And then it's time to bring the girls into their wonderful new room. They can't believe it! The room is very different. Now the room is bright with
35 lots of colours. There's a bright pink blind over the old fireplace. The girls' little models are in glass cases on the walls. Now everyone can see them. And lift up the cool sofa bed and it's a desk with everything they need for a small film studio – an animation station! The photos look great on the special wallpaper. And the blue cupboard is brilliant too. Then there's
40 another surprise. The girls have their own work stations but … open the cupboard in Freya's alcove and there's another table with a sewing machine. Hattie's got one too. "Thank you so much!" The girls love the room, everyone in the family loves the room. As the girls say, 'It's the best room ever!'

6

Take care

I can talk about the body, injuries and keeping fit.

1 ● Complete the labels for the parts of the body.

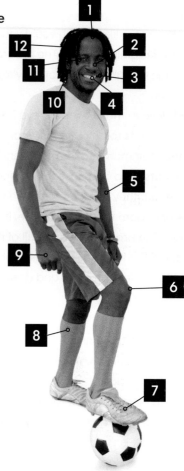

1 _hea_d
2 _ _ _ _ e
3 _ _ _ _ _ h
4 _ _ _ _ _ h
5 _ _ m
6 _ _ _ e
7 _ _ t
8 _ _ g
9 _ _ _ d
10 _ _ r
11 _ _ e
12 _ _ _ r

2 ● Find ten words from Exercise 1 in the word search. Which two words are NOT there?

V	Q	H	T	T	T	W	F	M	N
E	L	A	S	E	D	W	L	A	F
B	I	N	O	S	E	U	N	M	O
M	G	D	J	X	M	T	R	L	O
X	E	F	M	H	J	A	H	U	T
K	J	J	H	V	E	V	S	T	H
R	N	V	U	A	A	A	G	U	V
L	I	E	H	R	I	D	D	O	Y
H	N	V	E	M	C	R	I	O	P
B	H	G	M	O	U	T	H	B	J

3 ●● Choose the correct option.
1 Use your (brain)/ neck and think hard!
2 My *eyebrow* / *skin* went brown in the sun.
3 After the race my *heart* / *stomach* was going very fast.
4 Jack goes to the gym to get bigger *bones* / *muscles*.
5 My dad's hair is brown but his *ankle* / *beard* is white.
6 I can't eat any more. My *stomach* / *lips* is full.

4 ●● Complete the sentences with the correct words.

| shoulders   knee   ~~toes~~   fingers   elbow   bones

1 These shoes are too small. They hurt my _toes_ .
2 Children like to paint with their _____ – they don't like to use brushes.
3 My young sister likes sitting high up on my dad's _____ .
4 Drink a lot of milk and you get strong _____ that don't break.
5 I hurt my leg last week and I now can't bend my _____ .
6 I hit the desk with my arm and hurt my _____ when I fell.

5 ● WORD FRIENDS Match sentences 1–4 with pictures A–D.

1 | D | Mark hurt his back yesterday.
2 | ☐ | Emily cut her finger when she was cooking.
3 | ☐ | Jake twisted his ankle during the match.
4 | ☐ | Ellie broke her toe when she fell over.

6 ●● WORD FRIENDS Match the parts of the sentences.

1 | e | My brother keeps
2 | ☐ | We never play
3 | ☐ | I usually go
4 | ☐ | My friends and I do
5 | ☐ | My mum has

a private tennis lessons at the club.
b basketball at school.
c yoga at the leisure centre.
d swimming on Saturdays.
e fit by running every day.

7 ●● Choose the correct answers.

1 Grant has got blond hair but dark _____ .
   a elbows   (b) eyebrows   c ears
2 Jenny twisted her _____ while she was playing football.
   a bones   b heart   c knee
3 People who can't hear sometimes watch people's_____ .
   a lips   b nose   c teeth
4 I never _____ running before school.
   a keep   b go   c do
5 My uncle had a long _____ when he was a teenager.
   a beard   b hair   c arm
6 I haven't got very big _____ in my arms.
   a skin   b muscles   c fingers
7 I can carry my new leather bag over my _____ .
   a neck   b knee   c shoulder
8 My sister and I often _____ exercises at home to music.
   a have   b play   c do

8 ●●● Complete the text with the correct words.

| teeth   skin   ~~play~~   broke
| muscles   hurt   foot   does   has

Tennis players often get problems when they [1] _play_ tennis regularly. One of my friends [2]_____ lessons every week. She also [3]_____ lots of exercises and enters competitions nearly every weekend. She gets lots of injuries. She needs new shoes because she has a bad [4]_____ pain – that's because she jumps up and down a lot. She also [5]_____ her head last month because another player hit her with a ball! When she plays in the summer her [6]_____ often goes very red. Last year she even [7]_____ a bone in her ankle because she fell over! And once someone hit the ball right in her face and she broke two [8]_____ . She usually needs a warm bath after playing because all her [9]_____ are hurting.
You think tennis is a safe game but it's really quite dangerous!

I can talk about quantities of food.

1 ● Match pictures 1–10 with snacks a–j.

a ☐ hot dog
b ☐ sandwich
c ☐ [1] chocolate bar
d ☐ yoghurt
e ☐ fruit
f ☐ hamburger
g ☐ crisps
h ☐ nuts
i ☐ salad
j ☐ cake

2 ● Complete the table with the words below.

vegetable salami banana crisps sandwich salad fruit hot dog cake yoghurt bread food chocolate bar nut time sweet thing sugar meat chocolate burger chips

A	Countable nouns:
	vegetable _____ _____ _____ _____
	_____ _____ _____ _____ _____
B	Uncountable nouns:
	salami _____ _____ _____ _____
	_____ _____ _____ _____

3 ●● Order the words to make questions or sentences.

1 many / do / month / burgers / how / eat / you / a / ?
   How many burgers do you eat a month?

2 cake / too / eat / I / much
   _____

3 much / fridge / isn't / the / food / there / in
   _____

4 you / food / salt / how / your / put / much / on / do / ?
   _____

5 some / lunch / I've / for / got / crisps
   _____

6 should / fruit / lot / a / you / eat / of
   _____

7 got / they / chips / menu / haven't / any / the / on
   _____

8 sell / here / nuts / do / any / they / ?
   _____

4 ●● Complete the sentences with *some, any, much, many* and *a lot*.

1 A: How *many* sandwiches have you got today?
   B: I haven't got _____! We didn't have _____ bread at home so I brought _____ crisps and fruit instead.

2 A: How _____ time did you spend on your homework?
   B: I didn't spend _____ of time on it. It was quite easy.

3 I didn't get _____ answers right in that exercise. Only two!

4 I ate too _____ food at breakfast. I feel ill!

5 You've got _____ of snacks today!

5 ●●● Complete the text with the correct words.

Healthy living?

Are people healthy today? [1]*Some* doctors think we eat [2]_____ many unhealthy snacks. For example we eat a [3]_____ of burgers and hot dogs because they're quick to eat and they don't cost [4]_____ money. Schools are trying to encourage the students to eat healthy food. In some schools there aren't [5]_____ machines that sell snacks – not one! The students can't bring [6]_____ chocolate bars or crisps into school! They sell a lot [7]_____ healthy food in the cafeteria. There is always [8]_____ salad and a lot of fruit and vegetables but unfortunately not [9]_____ students eat them! [10]_____ students at these schools – not all – go out at lunchtime and buy a [11]_____ of unhealthy food like chips from local shops! So, [12]_____ many snacks do you eat every day?

I can find specific detail in a text and talk about sleeping habits.

1 WORD FRIENDS Complete the sentences with the correct verbs.

have   sleep   go   get x2   ~~fall~~   stay   wake

1 Sometimes I _fall_ asleep during my History lessons!
2 I know that I _____ dreams but I can never remember them.
3 I usually _____ in bed until lunchtime on Saturdays!
4 During the week I always need to _____ up at 7.30 but I need a clock to _____ me up on time.
5 I like to _____ ready for bed quite early and then read a book for half an hour.
6 My baby sister has to _____ to bed early and she hates it.
7 If I _____ badly, I can't work very well the next day.

2 Read the text and choose the best answers.

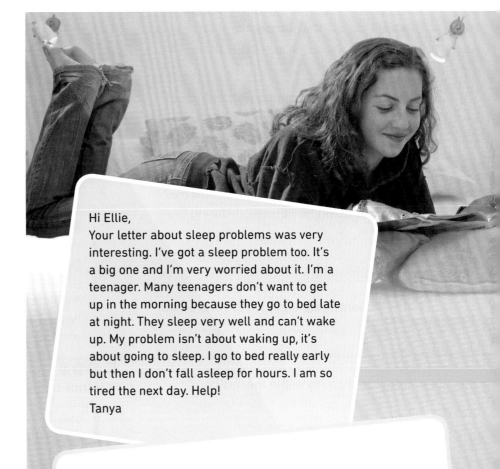

1 Tanya is writing to Ellie
   a about a letter she saw on her problem page.
   b about a sleep problem she has.
   c about some advice for another reader.
2 Tanya is worried because
   a she can't get up in the mornings.
   b she goes to bed too late in the evenings.
   c she can't go to sleep quickly at night.
3 Ellie thinks that
   a Tanya's problem is unusual.
   b Tanya's problem is normal.
   c Tanya's problem is interesting.
4 She believes the reason is that Tanya
   a works too hard.
   b argues with her parents.
   c thinks too much in bed.
5 Ellie advises Tanya to
   a have some quiet time before bed.
   b go to bed at different times.
   c see her doctor.

Hi Ellie,
Your letter about sleep problems was very interesting. I've got a sleep problem too. It's a big one and I'm very worried about it. I'm a teenager. Many teenagers don't want to get up in the morning because they go to bed late at night. They sleep very well and can't wake up. My problem isn't about waking up, it's about going to sleep. I go to bed really early but then I don't fall asleep for hours. I am so tired the next day. Help!
Tanya

Hi Tanya,
Don't worry! You're not the only one with this problem. Teenagers have a lot of things to worry about. They have a lot of exams and school work. Sometimes they have problems with friends or their parents. Perhaps when you go to bed you can't stop thinking about the problems and then you can't sleep. You need to relax before bedtime. Sometimes it's a good idea to have a warm bath or listen to some music – not too loud! Don't spend a long time talking to your friends before bed – just get some peace and quiet. It's also important to have the same routine – go to bed and get up at the same time. The body likes that! Some teenagers take tablets to help them fall asleep – not a good idea!! It's a bad habit. And don't worry about not sleeping – that makes it worse!
Ellie

I can talk about an event in the past and what was happening around it.

1 ● Complete the sentences with the positive Past Continuous form of the verbs.

wait   watch   play   walk   sleep   ~~dance~~   do

1 In the photograph Kate *was dancing* with Phil at his party.
2 At 5.00 this morning I _____ in my bed!
3 When you phoned me my parents _____ TV in the living room.
4 I _____ home from school when my dad drove past.
5 My sister _____ her guitar very loudly while I _____ my homework.
6 Sorry! We _____ for you in the park – not outside school.

2 ● Write the negative and question form of these sentences.

1 I was talking to Danny when you saw me.
I wasn't talking to Danny when you saw me.
Was I talking to Danny when you saw me?
2 Jake was doing his homework during the lesson.
_____
_____
_____
3 The students were eating chips and salad.
_____
_____
_____
4 You were playing well in the match.
_____
_____
_____
5 The teacher was explaining a difficult grammar point.
_____
_____
_____
6 You were having lunch when Sammy arrived.
_____
_____
_____

3 ●● Match the parts of the sentences.

1 [f] We were walking across the park
2 [ ] While I was eating my dinner
3 [ ] When I went downstairs
4 [ ] I fell asleep
5 [ ] My brother wasn't skiing
6 [ ] Jack was singing a song in the concert

a I dropped red sauce on my shirt.
b when he broke his ankle.
c dad was cooking breakfast.
d when he fell off the stage.
e while I was reading my book.
f when it started to rain.

4 ●● Complete the sentences with the Past Continuous or the Past Simple form of the verbs in brackets.

1 We *were eating* (eat) dinner outside when the rain *started* (start).
2 The students _____ (do) an exercise when the bell _____ (ring).
3 While I _____ (shop) on Saturday I _____ (meet) an old friend.
4 When I _____ (arrive) home my sister _____ (watch) a film on television.
5 I _____ (not look) when Paul _____ (fall) off his bicycle. I _____ (talk) to Marie.
6 What _____ (you/do) when I _____ (phone) you last night?

5 ●●● Complete the text with the correct past forms of the verbs.

look   go x2   see   not see   ~~wake~~   read
sit x2   chat x2   say   hurt   call   fall   ride

When I ¹*woke up* yesterday my head ²_____ so I ³_____ to see the doctor. I ⁴_____ in the waiting room and I ⁵_____ a magazine when suddenly someone ⁶_____ 'Hello Pat!'. I ⁷_____ up and it was Terry Marsden. I last ⁸_____ him five years ago at my first school! He ⁹_____ down beside me and we ¹⁰_____ for a long time. Last week he ¹¹_____ his horse when he ¹²_____ off! While we ¹³_____ the doctor ¹⁴_____ out 'Terry Marsden' and he ¹⁵_____ in to see the doctor. I ¹⁶_____ him later – I hope he was OK.

I can identify specific detail in a conversation and talk about illnesses.

1 Complete the words in the sentences.

1 I'm feeling **s**_ick_.
2 I've got a **h** _ _ **d** _ _ _ _ _ .
3 I've got a **s** _ _ **e t** _ _ _ _ **t**.
4 I'm **c** _ _ _ **h** _ **g**.
5 I'm **s** _ **e** _ _ **g**.
6 I've got a
 s _ _ **m** _ _ **h** _ _ _ **e**.
7 I've got hay **f** _ _ _ **r**.
8 I've got a food **a** _ _ _ **r** _ **y**.
9 I've got a high
 t _ **p** _ _ **t** _ _ **e**.
10 I've got the **f** _ _ .

2 Complete the sentences with the correct words from Exercise 1.

1 I ate too much and now I'm feeling _sick_.
2 In the summer I often sneeze because I get _____ .
3 I worked on my computer for a long time and now I've got a _____ .
4 If you get the _____ , you should stay in bed.
5 I can't eat or drink anything because I've got a very _____ .
6 I shouldn't eat fish because I've got a _____ .
7 Your face is hot and red. I think you've got a high _____ .

3 🔊 14 **Listen to Beth talking to Lloyd about a TV programme. Choose the correct answers.**

1 The singing competition was on TV on
 a Friday.
 ⓑ Saturday.
 c Monday.
2 What was wrong with Viva in the show?

A   B   C

3 Which is true?
 a Mark is always lucky in competitions.
 b Mark gets nervous.
 c Mark was sick during the show.
4 The winner was
 a Johnny.
 b Mark.
 c Viva.
5 The winner receives:

A   B   C

4 🔊 14 **Listen again and mark the sentences ✓ (right), ✗ (wrong) or ? (doesn't say).**

1 [?] Beth always watches singing competitions.
2 [ ] Lloyd had football training on Friday.
3 [ ] Johnny was very nervous.
4 [ ] Mark hurt his back in another competition.
5 [ ] The three singers make a record after the competition.
6 [ ] Beth and Lloyd can go to the concert in August.

I can talk about feeling ill and ask how someone is feeling.

1 Choose the correct option.

1 What's the *wrong* / (*matter*)?
2 *What* / *How* are you feeling?
3 I've got the *cold* / *flu*.
4 I feel *a headache* / *sick*.
5 My *back* / *temperature* hurts.
6 Sit *on* / *down*.
7 *Have* / *Take* some water.
8 You should stay *at the doctor* / *in bed*.
9 You should take some *tablet* / *medicine*.
10 You should *do* / *make* an appointment.
11 You should *go* / *take* to hospital.

2 Order the words to make sentences.

1 feel / I / terrible
   I feel terrible.
2 bad / I've / toothache / a / got
   _____
   _____
3 take / you / aspirin / an / should
   _____
   _____
4 should / an / dentist / with / you / appointment / make / the
   _____
   _____
5 in / you / bed / stay / should
   _____
   _____
   _____
6 broken / got / leg / a / I've
   _____
   _____
   _____

3 Complete the dialogues with the correct words.

| make an aspirin terrible |
| should feeling hay fever |
| sneezing What's feel ~~wrong~~ |

1 A: What's *wrong*?
   B: I _____ sick.
   A: You _____ go home.
2 A: How are you _____?
   B: I feel _____. My back hurts.
   A: You should _____ an appointment with the doctor.
3 A: _____ the matter?
   B: I've got a headache and I'm _____ a lot. I think I've got _____.
   A: You should have some water and then take _____.

4 🔊 15 Match gaps 1–6 with sentences a–f. Then listen and check.

A: ¹ *e*
B: I fell off my bicycle and my back hurts a bit.
A: ² ___
B: OK, thanks. I hit my head and that hurts too.
A: ³ ___
B: Thanks. Can I have some water with it?
A: ⁴ ___
B: Oh dear. That's making me feel sick now.
A: ⁵ ___
B: Oh and now I can't feel my leg!
A: ⁶ ___

a I've got some tablets for headaches. You should take one of these.
b OK. Forget the doctor. You should go to hospital!
c Come here and sit down for a moment.
d That's bad. You should make an appointment with your doctor.
e What's the matter? You look terrible.
f Sure. Here you are.

I can use phrasal verbs to talk about health.

1 Complete the sentences with the correct prepositions.

> out after off on up

1 I checked *out* my symptoms online.
2 I topped _____ my phone this morning.
3 My mum gave _____ drinking coffee two weeks ago.
4 David doesn't get _____ very well with Tom.
5 Why don't you take _____ swimming? It's a great sport.
6 The nurses looked _____ me very well when I was in hospital.
7 I usually hang _____ with my mates after school.
8 Something's going _____ in town. There are lots of police cars.
9 I found _____ the name of the tablets you need.
10 Grant and Lily aren't speaking. They fell _____ last week.
11 The milk went _____ so I threw it away.
12 Where did you pick _____ that cold?

2 Replace the underlined words with the correct phrasal verbs from Exercise 1.

1 I <u>discovered</u> that Jan and I lived in the same town when we were babies. *found out*
2 My dad <u>took care of</u> my mum when she was ill. _____
3 My brother <u>started</u> football last year. _____
4 Who do you <u>spend time</u> with at weekends? _____
5 What was <u>happening</u> outside school this morning? _____
6 I <u>stopped</u> dancing classes when I hurt my leg. _____
7 I must <u>consult</u> the train timetable for tomorrow. _____
8 I <u>had an argument</u> with Rosa last week. _____
9 Where did you <u>put more money on</u> your phone? _____
10 I kept the milk for too long and it <u>started to smell</u>! _____
11 I <u>was good friends</u> with my brother when I was young. _____
12 Danny <u>got</u> a cold when he stayed with his friend. _____

3 Choose the correct answers.

1 What's _____ on outside?
  a doing   ⓑ going   c taking
2 I dropped the pencil and the teacher _____ it up.
  a caught   b found   c picked
3 Mum _____ up coffee because she got a lot of headaches.
  a fell   b gave   c made
4 My sister and I _____ out last week because she broke my phone.
  a fell   b went   c picked
5 Why don't you _____ out this website?
  a look   b find   c check
6 Bread _____ off after three or four days.
  a makes   b goes   c gives
7 Brad started to _____ out with some friends from his new school.
  a get   b look   c hang
8 Chris _____ up football last year.
  a took   b topped   c got

4 Match the parts of the sentences.

1 [h] I don't get
2 [ ] Let's hang
3 [ ] Penny wants to give
4 [ ] Did you find
5 [ ] This bread went
6 [ ] I'd like to take
7 [ ] I looked
8 [ ] Before you buy that you should check

a out at the café after college.
b out the new clothes shop in the mall.
c off two days ago!
d out how much the medicine costs?
e up chocolate for a month!
f after my brother a lot when he was a baby.
g up a new hobby soon.
h on with people who are selfish.

6.8 SELF-ASSESSMENT

☺☺ = I understand and can help a friend.　　☹ = I understand but have some questions.

☺ = I understand and can do it by myself.　　☹☹ = I do not understand.

		☺☺	☺	☹	☹☹	Need help?	Now try ...
6.1	Vocabulary					Students' Book pp. 70–71 Workbook pp. 66–67	Ex. 1–3, p. 75
6.2	Grammar					Students' Book p. 72 Workbook p. 68	Ex. 4–5, p. 75
6.3	Reading					Students' Book p. 73 Workbook p. 69	
6.4	Grammar					Students' Book p. 74 Workbook p. 70	
6.5	Listening					Students' Book p. 75 Workbook p. 71	
6.6	Speaking					Students' Book p. 76 Workbook p. 72	Ex. 6, p. 75
6.7	English in Use					Students' Book p. 77 Workbook p. 73	

6.1　I can talk about the body, injuries and keeping fit.
6.2　I can talk about quantities of food.
6.3　I can find specific detail in a text and talk about sleeping habits.
6.4　I can talk about an event in the past and what was happening around it.
6.5　I can identify specific detail in a conversation and talk about illnesses.
6.6　I can talk about feeling ill and ask about how someone is feeling.
6.7　I can use phrasal verbs to talk about health.

New words I learned (the words you most want to remember from this unit)	**Expressions and phrases I liked** (any expressions or phrases you think sound nice, useful or funny)	**English I heard or read outside class** (e.g. from websites, books, adverts, films, music)

Vocabulary

1 Complete the words from the descriptions.

1 Your food goes here: **s** _ _ _ _ _ _
2 This sometimes goes red in the sun:
   s _ _ _ _
3 Men have this when they don't shave:
   b _ _ _ _
4 Your foot joins your leg here: **a** _ _ _ _ _
5 When you exercise a lot these get very
   strong: **m** _ _ _ _ _ _
6 The dentist checks these every year:
   t _ _ _ _ _

2 Choose the correct answers.

1 I try to eat well and _____ fit.
   a have   **b** do   **c** keep
2 I usually _____ to bed at 10.30 to get
   eight hours of sleep.
   a go   **b** make   **c** sleep
3 I've got a _____ for my sister's birthday
   with her name on it.
   a nuts   **b** cake   **c** yoghurt
4 It's a good idea to eat _____ every day,
   even just one apple.
   a crisps   **b** sandwiches **c** fruit
5 Doctors say it's important to _____
   regular exercise.
   a make   **b** do   **c** play
6 Would you like your chicken with a _____
   or chips?
   a beef burger **b** salad   **c** hot dog

3 Complete the sentences with the correct
words.

allergy   flu   hay   headache
temperature   throat

1 He needs to see the doctor because his
   _____ is very high.
2 I can't eat that. I've got a(n) _____ to
   nuts.
3 In summer I get terrible _____ fever.
4 The music at the concert was very loud
   and I got a(n) _____ .
5 We shouted a lot at the football match
   and now I've got a sore _____ .
6 Olly has to stay in bed because he's got
   the _____ .

Grammar

4 Complete the sentences with the correct words.

1 How _____ water do you drink every day?
2 There aren't _____ students in the
   classroom. Only two.
3 I watched too much television last night and
   I didn't do _____ work! Nothing!
4 A _____ of people don't do any exercise
   and get ill.
5 Did you eat all the fruit? There _____ any left.
6 I answered _____ of the questions but not
   many.

5 Make sentences in the Past Simple and the Past
Continuous.

1 where / you / go / when / I / see / you / this
   morning / ?
   _____
2 Hannah / read / a book / when / Gary / call /
   at her house
   _____
3 I / not work / when / Dave / come / to visit us
   _____
4 you / wait / at the bus stop / when / it / start /
   to rain / ?
   _____
5 the teacher / shout at us / because we /
   not concentrate / in class today
   _____
6 you / have / dinner / when / I / phone / you
   earlier / ?
   _____

Speaking language practice

6 Complete the dialogues with one word in
each gap.

1 **A:** What's the _____?
   B: I've _____ toothache.
   A: You _____ go to the dentist.
2 **A:** How are you _____?
   B: My back _____.
   A: You should make an _____ with your
        doctor.
3 **A:** What's _____?
   B: I _____ sick.
   A: Sit _____ and have _____ water.

1 Match words 1–4 with photos A–D.

1 `B` buffalo   3 ☐ haggis
2 ☐ crowd   4 ☐ chess

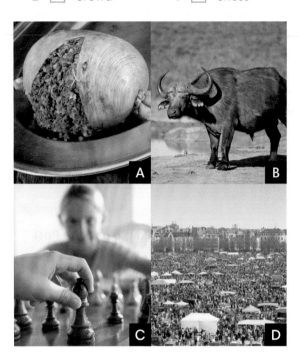

2 Choose the correct option.

1 I often *do* / *play* chess with my friend after school.
2 My brother fell *down* / *off* his horse last year and went to hospital.
3 If you think *hard* / *hardly*, you will find the answer, I'm sure!
4 They played football in the rain this morning and *got* / *went* very dirty.
5 In the swimming competition, I had to *run* / *race* against some very fast people.
6 In this sport, we need a *team* / *pair* of four people.

3 Match the pairs of sentences.

1 `c` Jack takes part in lots of competitions.
2 ☐ Rob isn't very fit.
3 ☐ Pete is really muddy.
4 ☐ Olly plays a hybrid sport – football tennis.

a He was playing with his sister in the field.
b He needs to be good at two sports!
c He earns a lot of money when he wins.
d He needs to do more exercise.

4 Label photos 1–6 with the correct words.

artist   boxer   ~~dancer~~   runner   swimmer   trainer

dancer _____ _____

_____ _____ _____

5 Complete the dialogues with the correct words.

alternative   backwards   directions   encourage   ~~imaginative~~   slanted

1 A: This is a very good short story.
    B: Yes, Katy is very *imaginative* .
2 A: This table isn't straight.
    B: You're right. It's _____!
3 A: Let's meet at the leisure centre.
    B: I don't know where it is. Can you give me _____?
4 A: He's swimming very slowly.
    B: Yes, I think he's going _____!
5 A: In our country, they're using the wind to make energy.
    B: Yes, it's a good _____ to oil.
6 A: You must enter the competition. You're the best!
    B: Thanks. You always _____ me.

6 Complete the words in the sentences.

1 We can't play table tennis now – there's a hole in the **net** .
2 The man put the little girl on his **s**_____**s** so she could see the match.
3 What **p**_____ did you win in the competition?
4 We always **c**_____ loudly when our football team wins.
5 A table tennis ball isn't **h**_____ . It's very light.
6 I burned a lot of **c**_____ at the gym this morning. Now I can have a biscuit!

7 Read the video script. Underline any words or phrases you don't know and find their meaning in your dictionary.

Unusual sports

Part 1

Do you like sport? Perhaps you want to do or watch something a bit different? OK. Here are some ideas. These are definitely not Olympic sports … yet.

This is the World Alternative Games. It's on for three weeks and there are thirty

5 very unusual sports. There's a race between men and horses. There's swimming in the mud and banana cycling.

There's another interesting sport too. Here the runners are getting ready for their race. What's the event? It's backwards running. It isn't new. The Chinese did this ten thousand years ago. It became popular in the USA in the last century.

10 Boxers, dancers and trainers did backwards running.

It's very good for your back and your stomach. It also makes you slim because you use lots of calories. People say it makes you taller and cleverer. That's because you need to use the right side of your brain. It looks funny. It isn't easy – it's hard to look over your shoulder – but some runners say it's quite relaxing.

15 Here's some very important advice. If you take up this sport – don't do it on the streets. Practise in a park.

Part 2

There's another unusual sport that is getting very popular. I'm sure you know table tennis or 'ping pong'. This is table tennis that looks a bit wrong – it's 'wrong

20 pong'. In 'wrong pong', you play table tennis on different sorts of tables. Here there are three players and three parts to the table. Two artists started 'wrong pong' in 2010. They were bored and wanted to try something different. They were very creative and imaginative. First they made a table that was moving. They thought art and sport could go together. They believed that sports must

25 change and must be interesting for everyone.

You can also play wrong pong on slanted tables. They can go up and down and in different directions. And sometimes there are one, two or three nets. There's a round table for three people. You can even play on one that has things on it, like paint – you don't know where the ball will go. When you play this game,

30 you have to think differently and it's great fun. Traditional table tennis players also love wrong pong because it's encouraging lots of people to start the sport. There's even a world cup for wrong pong – a very special prize.

Part 3

And finally here is a very, very strange race. What are these people getting

35 ready for? It's a wife carrying race.

The racers are all very strong. They know what to do and they practise a lot. But this is new for Mike and Steph. They try to do the same but – oops – he falls off. So, they decide to do it a different way. This race started in Finland in the 1990s but now it happens all over the world. It's called a 'wife carrying race' but

40 the couple don't need to be married. Usually the man carries the woman. But here for the first time a woman is going to carry a man. Mike is 'the wife' – and a very heavy one. It isn't easy. People throw water at them and some of the 'wives' fall off. The winners get a prize and everyone cheers. Mike and Steph are very slow. They're tired and wet but finally they finish. This time Mike is running.

Shopping around

I can talk about shops and what they sell.

1 ● Use the letters to write the names of types of shops that sell the things from the pictures.

1 STEEGAWNN'S
newsagent's

2 HOKOBOSP
_____

3 OHES OHSP
_____

4 RUTHBEC'S
_____

5 TROFSIL'S
_____

6 EKRABY
_____

7 CRERENOGREG'S
_____

8 OLESTCH HPOS
_____

9 CHAPRAMY
_____

2 ●● Complete the sentences with the correct words.

> butcher's   shoe shop   florist's   ~~bakery~~   newsagent's
> clothes shop   pharmacy   greengrocer's

1 We need some bread. Can you go to the *bakery*?
2 I bought some new jeans at the _____.
3 They sell lovely apples at the _____.
4 I want a magazine and some chocolate from the _____.
5 Please get some chicken from the _____.
6 I need some new boots. I must go to the _____.
7 I've got a bad headache. Can you get me some tablets from the _____?
8 It's mum's birthday tomorrow. Let's get her some flowers from the _____.

3 WORD FRIENDS **Complete the sentences with the correct words.**

| bunch | ~~jar~~ | bottle | packet | can | box |

1 I dropped a *jar* of marmalade and it broke.
2 I can't open this _____ of crisps. Can you help me?
3 We should put this _____ of roses in some water.
4 Jamie gave me a _____ of chocolates yesterday. They're very good!
5 I always take a _____ of water when I go running.
6 I'd like a _____ of cola, please.

4 **Match containers 1–8 with items a–h. Then label the pictures below.**

1 [c] a loaf of   a jam
2 [ ] a bar of   b flowers
3 [ ] a jar of   c bread
4 [ ] a packet of   d apples
5 [ ] a bunch of   e chocolate
6 [ ] a bottle of   f crisps
7 [ ] a box of   g lemonade
8 [ ] a bag of   h matches

A

a loaf of bread

B

C

_____

D

_____

E

_____

F

_____

G

_____

H

_____

5 ●● **Choose the correct answers.**

1 I need some oranges but the _____ is closed.
   a pharmacy   b shoe shop
   ⓒ greengrocer's
2 I bought three _____ of chocolate this morning.
   a cans   b bars   c bunches
3 If you get a _____ of bread, I can make some sandwiches.
   a loaf   b packet   c box
4 We got these lovely flowers at the _____.
   a bakery   b florist's   c butcher's
5 I can't make a cup of coffee because the _____'s empty.
   a jar   b bar   c bottle
6 Our _____ sells shampoo.
   a greengrocer's   b clothes shop
   c pharmacy
7 You shouldn't eat so many _____ of crisps! They're bad for you.
   a jars   b packets   c boxes
8 There's a new _____ in town which sells beautiful dresses.
   a clothes shop   b shoe shop
   c newsagent's

6 ●●● **Complete Maria's note for Brian with the correct words.**

| box | newsagent's | ~~greengrocer's~~ | bakery |
| loaf | butcher's | packets | jar | bottles | bag |

Hi Brian!

Thanks for doing the shopping today. We need lots of things for the party tomorrow. First can you go to the ¹*greengrocer's* and get some oranges and a big ²_____ of apples, please. Then go to the ³_____. We need five big ⁴_____ of crisps for the party and a magazine for me, please! Can you also get a ⁵_____ of cream cakes from the ⁶_____ in the High Street – and a white ⁷_____ too? I love their bread! If you get a chicken from the ⁸_____, I can cook it and use it for sandwiches tomorrow. I think our friends drink coffee, so a ⁹_____ of coffee too, please – and three or four ¹⁰_____ of lemonade.

I think that's all! I hope you can carry it all!

Maria x

I can compare things.

1 ● Complete the sentences with the correct form of the adjectives in brackets.

1 This film is <u>*older*</u> (old) than that one.
2 These flowers are _____ (nice) than the ones in the florist's.
3 It's _____ (warm) today than it was yesterday.
4 Which is _____ (long) river in the world?
5 The phone signal is _____ (good) here than inside the house.
6 I bought _____ (expensive) bike in the shop.
7 Emily is _____ (happy) person I know.
8 My _____ (bad) mark this year was for Maths!

2 ●● Make three sentences for the pairs of adjectives 1–4.

1 short/tall
A is *shorter than* B.
B is *taller than* A.
C is *the tallest* person in my family.

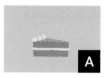  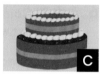

2 small/big
A is _____ B.
B is _____ A.
C is _____ cake in the shop.

3 cheap/expensive
A is _____ B.
B is _____ A.
C is _____ book in the shop.

4 sad/happy
B is _____ A.
A is _____ B.
C is _____ student in the class.

3 ●● Complete the second sentence with *as … as …* so that it means the same as the first sentence.

1 I'm taller than my brother.
My brother isn't *as tall as me*.
2 It's colder in Scotland than it is here.
It isn't _____ .
3 This programme is more interesting than the programme last night.
The programme last night wasn't _____ .
4 Your jeans were more expensive than mine.
My jeans weren't _____ .
5 My new bed is more comfortable than my old one.
My old bed wasn't _____ .
6 My sister's bedroom is tidier than mine.
My bedroom isn't _____ .

4 ●●● Complete the email with the correct forms of the adjectives in brackets.

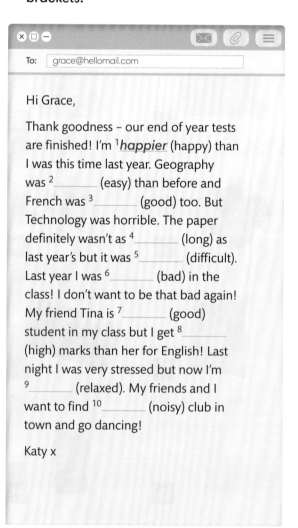

To: grace@hellomail.com

Hi Grace,

Thank goodness – our end of year tests are finished! I'm ¹*happier* (happy) than I was this time last year. Geography was ² _____ (easy) than before and French was ³ _____ (good) too. But Technology was horrible. The paper definitely wasn't as ⁴ _____ (long) as last year's but it was ⁵ _____ (difficult). Last year I was ⁶ _____ (bad) in the class! I don't want to be that bad again! My friend Tina is ⁷ _____ (good) student in my class but I get ⁸ _____ (high) marks than her for English! Last night I was very stressed but now I'm ⁹ _____ (relaxed). My friends and I want to find ¹⁰ _____ (noisy) club in town and go dancing!

Katy x

I can find specific detail in a text and talk about a department store.

1 Complete the sentences with the correct words.

shoppers   trolley   multi-screen cinema   ~~department store~~   escalator   food court   public toilets   car park

1 We went to the *department store* and bought some new clothes, some things for the kitchen and a lamp for my bedroom.
2 In the shopping centre the _____ wasn't working so we had to use the stairs.
3 Dad bought so many things in the supermarket that he needed a big _____ to carry it all.
4 The _____ was nearly empty so it was easy to find a space for the car.
5 The new shopping centre has thousands of _____ every day.
6 There's a new sandwich bar in the _____ where we can have lunch today.
7 The _____ at the new shopping centre are always very clean and are like those in a hotel!
8 There are ten films showing at the _____. I'm sure there's one you want to see!

2 Read the text. Mark the sentences ✓ (right), ✗ (wrong) or ? (doesn't say).

1 [?] Selfridges is the biggest department store in London.
2 [ ] Harry Selfridge wasn't from England.
3 [ ] Before Selfridges people bought lots of things they did not need.
4 [ ] In Selfridges it was easier for shoppers to see things.
5 [ ] Selfridges has more windows than other stores in Oxford Street.
6 [ ] Nothing in Selfridges is very expensive.

3 Match the words from the text with definitions 1–6.

designer   counter   ~~chore~~   scene
customer   motto

1 A job which is boring but needs to be done, like housework: *chore*
2 A person who plans the look of artistic things: _____
3 A salesperson stands behind this in many shops: _____
4 A saying that tells us something about a company or school: _____
5 A person who buys something in a shop: _____
6 A view or a picture: _____

The best department store in the world?

Oxford Street in London is well-known for its big department stores. Selfridges is one of them. It is named after Harry Selfridge, an American man who came to London with his family in 1909. He opened his new store on 15 March and it immediately became very popular. But why was it so successful?

There were many reasons. At that time shoppers bought things because they needed to, not because they wanted to. Harry Selfridge wanted to change that. He wanted to make shopping more fun, more of an adventure than a chore. He wanted people to enjoy going round his department store. So he didn't keep all the items in cupboards or on shelves, he put them on counters for people to see. The shoppers could look and touch things and choose what they wanted. And Selfridge's motto was 'The Customer is always right!' This idea made the shopper more important than the seller.

The store was also an amazing building. It had a garden on the roof! And, of course there were the wonderful shop windows. People came to Oxford Street just to look at the scenes in the windows. He employed some of the best designers in Europe and even today Selfridge's windows are in magazines all over the world – especially at Christmas.

Harry Selfridge changed shopping for everyone with his new store. It isn't the cheapest place to go shopping but it is certainly one of the most beautiful and interesting stores in the world!

I can talk about intentions and arrangements.

1 ● **Complete the sentences with the correct form of *going to* and the verbs in brackets.**

1 I *'m going to phone* (phone) Laura later to ask about her exam.

2 We _____ (look) round the new shopping centre on Saturday morning.

3 _____ (your mother/get) a new car soon?

4 I _____ (not become) a doctor. I want to be a research scientist.

5 Dad _____ (get) a bigger computer for the family next month.

6 _____ (you/email) Sonia about the party?

2 ●● **Complete the sentences with the correct Present Continuous form of the verbs.**

1 My mum*'s starting* (start) a new job on Monday.

2 It's my birthday on Saturday and I _____ (have) a party at my house in the evening.

3 _____ (you/fly) from Gatwick or Heathrow this weekend?

4 A famous actor _____ (open) the new shopping mall on 16 June.

5 Sorry, my mistake! We _____ (not meet) Jane at 6 but at 6.30.

6 Jake is really pleased. He _____ (play) in the school football match on Friday.

3 ●● **Complete the sentences with the *going to* or Present Continuous form of the verbs in bold.**

1 My plan is to **ask** dad to lend me some money for a new laptop.
I *'m going to ask dad* to lend me some money for a new laptop.

2 The arrangement is for Leo and me to **catch** the same train tomorrow.
Leo and I are _____ the same train tomorrow.

3 I want to **have** a quick shower and then go out with Geoff.
I'm _____ a quick shower and then go out with Geoff.

4 Jack's aim is to **work** hard for the next exams.
Jack is _____ hard for the next exams.

5 The arrangement is for Dan and Kevin to **arrive** at 7 not at 8!
Dan and Kevin aren't _____ at 8 but at 7.

6 Miss Baines agreed to **give** me a piano lesson on Thursday at 4.30.
Miss Baines is _____ me a piano lesson on Thursday at 4.30.

7 Do you plan to **spend** a lot of money at the shopping centre on Saturday?
Are you _____ a lot of money at the shopping centre on Saturday?

8 I don't want to **read** my book this evening because I'm too busy.
I'm not _____ my book this evening because I'm too busy.

4 ●●● **Complete the message with the *going to* or Present Continuous form of the verbs.**

| play make ~~have~~ go bring |
| check out buy show do |

Nicky,

This is just a quick message about arranging to go out next week. My diary is quite full! I ¹*'m having* a driving lesson on Monday at 4.30 after college and on Tuesday I ² _____ shopping with my gran at 4.00. She ³ _____ my birthday present and she wants me to choose it! I ⁴ _____ her round the new shopping centre in the High Street. Then on Wednesday I ⁵ _____ in a tennis match at lunchtime and in the evening I think Sally ⁶ _____ round some photos from her holiday to show me – if she's got time. How about Thursday? ⁷ _____ you _____ anything on Thursday after school? I really need some summer tops so I ⁸ _____ some shopping websites – but I can do that any time so let me know if you are free. Right, now I ⁹ _____ some sandwiches and watch some TV.

Speak soon x

I can identify specific detail in a conversation and talk about money.

1 Complete the words from the descriptions.

1 A container where children put money to save it: p*iggybank*

2 Money that parents give children every week:
p _ _ _ _ _ _ m _ _ _ _ _

3 The cost of something in the shop: p _ _ _ _

4 A time when things are cheaper in the shops:
s _ _ _ _

5 You keep your money in this when you go out:
w _ _ _ _ _ _ / p _ _ _ _ _

6 The money that the assistant gives you back when you buy something: c _ _ _ _ _ _

2 WORD FRIENDS **Match the parts of the sentences.**

1 [e] When I was a child I
2 ☐ I went shopping yesterday and I
3 ☐ My uncle has a job in London and he
4 ☐ Kenny was very kind and he
5 ☐ Last year my dad was careful and he
6 ☐ Last month I lent Paul some money and yesterday he
7 ☐ My sister never has much money and often

a spent a lot of money in the expensive clothes shop in the town centre.
b borrows some from me to go shopping.
c lent me some money to buy a concert ticket.
d saved enough money to buy a new car.
e got £8 pocket money every week.
f paid me back.
g earns a £1,000 a week.

3 🔊 16 **Listen to a conversation between Jenny and Harry. Mark the sentences ✓ (right) or ✗ (wrong).**

1 ✓ Jenny doesn't want to stay in a hotel.
2 ☐ Jenny needs to buy a new computer.
3 ☐ Jenny needs some money immediately.
4 ☐ She is worried about paying Harry back the money.
5 ☐ Harry suggests she does some babysitting.
6 ☐ Jenny accepts Harry's offer of money.

4 🔊 16 **Listen again and choose the correct answers.**

1 Which concert does Jenny want to go to?
a Ellie Goulding
b Sam Smith
ⓒ One Direction

2 When are Jenny's exams?
a in March
b in May
c in June

3 The tickets are going on sale at
a one o'clock.
b two o'clock.
c three o'clock.

4 Who is going to buy the tickets?
a Alexa
b Olly
c Jenny

5 How much does Jenny earn from babysitting now?
a £10
b £50
c £15

6 Where did Jenny live before?
a in London
b in the USA
c in Paris

I can shop for clothes and other things.

1 Choose the correct option.

1 This coat is too big. Have you got a smaller (one)/ ones?
2 Do you want the cheap tickets or the expensive one / ones?
3 I love chicken sandwiches but I don't like cheese one / ones.
4 This phone is very old. I'd like a newer one / ones.
5 My laptop isn't as big as this one / ones.
6 This phone is better than my last one / ones.

2 Complete the sentences with the correct words.

| much   take   sale   ~~help~~   size   forget

1 Can I _help_ you?
2 These ones are on _____.
3 What _____ are you?
4 How _____ is it?
5 Don't _____ your change.
6 I'll _____ them.

3 Order the words to make sentences or questions.

1 a / looking / jacket / for / I'm
   I'm looking for a jacket.
2 is / how / it / much / ?
   _____
   _____
3 this / please / try / I / on / can / ?
   _____
   _____
4 rooms / there / the / over / changing / are
   _____
   _____
5 it / have / colour / got / another / you / in / ?
   _____
   _____
6 are / these / small / too
   _____
   _____

4 Match questions 1–6 with answers a–f.

1 [a] Can I help you?
2 [ ] How much are these?
3 [ ] Can I try these on, please?
4 [ ] What size are you?
5 [ ] Have you got them in a smaller size?
6 [ ] Are they the right size?

a I'm looking for some jeans.
b They're too big.
c I'm sorry, we haven't.
d I'm size twelve.
e Sure. The changing rooms are over there.
f They're in the sale. They're fifteen pounds.

5 🔊 17 Match gaps 1–8 with sentences a–h. Then listen and check.

A: Hi there. Can I help you?
B: ¹ _g_
A: These ones are in the sale.
B: ² ____
A: They're twenty-five pounds. Do you like the brown ones?
B: ³ ____
A: Yes. What size are you?
B: ⁴ ____
A: Here you are. Size twelve.
B: ⁵ ____
A: Sure. The changing rooms are over there.
B: ⁶ ____
A: Try these. They're size fourteen.
B: ⁷ ____
A: Great. They look really nice.
B: ⁸ ____
A: Thanks. Don't forget your change.

a Mm … Have you got them in black?
b Thanks. Oh yes, that's much better.
c Yes. I'll take them. Twenty-five pounds? Here you are.
d They're nice. How much are they?
e Twelve.
f Thanks. … Oh dear. They're too small.
g Yes. I'm looking for some jeans.
h Great. Can I try them on?

I can write notes and messages to make arrangements.

1 Complete the sentences with the correct words.

> hope should Let's Perhaps Help going Let
> leaving Can Would planning can't there

A Greeting

Hi Rita,

B The information you want the other person to know.

I'm ¹*going* to the beach.

² _____ ! My computer isn't working.

I'm really busy – I ³ _____ come.

The train is really late.

C A request, offer or invitation

⁴ _____ you like to come?

⁵ _____ you help?

⁶ _____ you could come round after school?

Please wait for me.

D Arrangements

I ⁷ _____ be outside my house at two o'clock.

⁸ _____ meet at the entrance to the park at 12.30.

We're ⁹ _____ at two o'clock.

I'm ¹⁰ _____ to be at the tennis club at 7.30.

E Ending

See you ¹¹ _____ /soon.

¹² _____ me know.

I ¹³ _____ you can come/help.

Love

2 Use phrases from Exercise 1 and the information below to write short notes.

1 To Sara from Anna. Me and Danny – beach this afternoon. You/come? Leave/two o'clock. Pick up/ outside house?

Hi Sara,

Danny and I are going to the beach this afternoon. Would you like to come? We're leaving about two o'clock. Perhaps we could pick you up outside your house?

Let me know.

Love, Anna

2 To Anna from Sara. Yes, please/outside house 2.05. See/soon.

_____

_____

_____

3 To Dean from Mick. Computer/not working. You/help? Come round after school?

_____

_____

3 Read the information (A) and the email (B). Then complete the information in Lola's notes (C).

Come to Jake's eighteenth birthday barbecue

on Sunday at 1 Wood Lane.
Starts at 12.30 and continues until ????
Please bring a plate of food –
sausages/sandwiches?
Tell me if you can come by Thursday.

Jake

A

From: Jake;
To: Lola;

Hope you can come, Lola. Can you tell Alexa about it too, please? I haven't got her email address and she's off school at the moment. Dave and some others are meeting at the bus stop to get the 12.15 bus. You could meet up there?

B

Lola's Notes

Barbecue

Person having barbecue: ¹ *Jake*

Reason: ² _____

Day: ³ _____

Time: ⁴ _____

Take: ⁵ _____

Travel by: ⁶ _____

Meet up at: ⁷ _____

C

4 Use the information in Lola's notes to write a note to Alexa about the barbecue.

a Use the phrases from Exercise 1 in your note.

b Start and finish your note correctly.

For each learning objective, tick (✓) the box that best matches your ability.

☺☺ = I understand and can help a friend.   ☹ = I understand but have some questions.

☺ = I understand and can do it by myself.   ☹☹ = I do not understand.

		☺☺	☺	☹	☹☹	Need help?	Now try ...
7.1	Vocabulary					Students' Book pp. 82–83 Workbook pp. 78–79	Ex. 1–3, p. 87
7.2	Grammar					Students' Book p. 84 Workbook p. 80	Ex. 4–5, p. 87
7.3	Reading					Students' Book p. 85 Workbook p. 81	
7.4	Grammar					Students' Book p. 86 Workbook p. 82	
7.5	Listening					Students' Book p. 87 Workbook p. 83	
7.6	Speaking					Students' Book p. 88 Workbook p. 84	Ex. 6, p. 87
7.7	Writing					Students' Book p. 89 Workbook p. 85	

7.1   I can talk about shops and what they sell.
7.2   I can compare things.
7.3   I can find specific detail in a text and talk about a department store.
7.4   I can talk about intentions and arrangements.
7.5   I can identify specific detail in a conversation and talk about money.
7.6   I can shop for clothes and other things.
7.7   I can write notes and messages to make arrangements.

What can you remember from this unit?

New words I learned (the words you most want to remember from this unit)	**Expressions and phrases I liked** (any expressions or phrases you think sound nice, useful or funny)	**English I heard or read** **outside class** (e.g. from websites, books, adverts, films, music)

Vocabulary

1 Complete the questions and answers.

1 A: Where can you buy a **b** _ _ _ _ _ _ of flowers?
  B: At the **f** _ _ _ _ _ _ _ ' _ .
2 A: Where can you buy a **l** _ _ _ of bread?
  B: At the **b** _ _ _ _ _ _ .
3 A: Where can you buy a **b** _ _ of apples?
  B: At the **g** _ _ _ _ _ _ _ _ _ _ ' _ .
4 A: Where can you buy a **b** _ _ _ _ _ of shampoo?
  B: At the **p** _ _ _ _ _ _ _ .
5 A: Where can you buy a **b** _ _ of chocolate and a magazine?
  B: At the **n** _ _ _ _ _ _ _ _ _ _ ' _ .
6 A: Where can you buy a **p** _ _ _ of boots?
  B: At the **s** _ _ _ _ **s** _ _ _ _ .

2 Complete the sentences with the correct words.

> court   department   escalator   toilets
> trolley   shopper

1 The _____ wasn't working so we used the stairs.
2 We had a lot of food to buy and our _____ was full.
3 We had a meal in the food _____ .
4 I like _____ stores because they have a lot of different things.
5 Where are the public _____ , please?
6 I was the last _____ in the supermarket!

3 Complete the sentences with the correct words.

1 My young sister gets five pounds _____ money a week from our parents.
2 I think you gave me the wrong _____ . I gave you ten pounds.
3 Excuse me, how _____ are these jeans?
4 I bought this jumper last week in the winter _____ and it was very cheap.
5 Did you put your money in a _____ bank when you were a child?
6 Oh no! I left my _____ in the shop. There was a lot of money in it!

Grammar

4 Complete the sentences with the correct comparative or superlative form of the adjectives in brackets.

1 Your book is _____ than my novel. (interesting)
2 The new department store is _____ than the old one was. (big)
3 *The Hobbit* was _____ film I saw last year. (enjoyable)
4 My bed isn't _____ as my sister's. (comfortable)
5 Mum's laptop was _____ than the one in the shop. (cheap)

5 Make sentences or questions with *going to* or the Present Continuous form of the verbs.

1 how much money / you / spend on Saturday / ?
_____
2 my dad / look for / a new job soon
_____
3 I / play tennis / with Erica at 2.30 today
_____
4 when / you / arrive back / from holiday / ?
_____
5 I / try / to do my homework this evening
_____

Speaking language practice

6 Match sentences a–e with gaps 1–5.

A: Can I help you?
B: ¹ _____
A: These ones are on sale.
B: ² _____
A: They're forty-five pounds.
B: ³ _____
A: They're a thirty-eight.
B: ⁴ _____
A: Certainly. Here's a seat.
B: ⁵ _____

a They're fine. Thanks. I'll take them.
b What size are the brown ones?
c Can I try them on?
d I'm looking for some boots.
e How much are they?

1 Complete the words from the descriptions.

1 You can relax in the water here: **spa**

2 People buy and sell things here:
   a _ _ _ _ _ _

3 You sail across the sea in this: **y** _ _ _ _

4 You do this regularly, e.g. every day:
   h _ _ _ _ _

5 This is the top part of your face:
   f _ _ _ _ _ _ _

6 Dead people are in this place:
   c _ _ _ _ _ _ _

7 It takes you to different floors in a
   building: **l** _ _ _

8 This persuades us to buy things, e.g.,
   on TV: **a** _ _ _ _ _ _ _ _ _ _ _

2 Complete the sentences with the correct
form of the verbs.

> celebrate ~~operate~~ own put start stay

1 This company only *operates* in Europe, not
   in the USA.

2 My dad _____ his camera for sale on eBay.

3 My brother wants to _____ a new life in
   Australia.

4 My granny doesn't like things to change
   – she always wants things to _____ the
   same.

5 My dad _____ two cars – one is very old
   and one is new.

6 I usually _____ my birthday at a restaurant
   with my friends and family.

3 Complete the sentences with the correct
form of words from Exercises 1 and 2.

1 Put your hand on Mark's *forehead* – I think
   he's ill because he's very hot.

2 I passed all my exams and to _____ my
   mum is going to pay for a weekend at a
   _____ !

3 Jake has got some very bad _____ – one
   of them is watching films until late at night.

4 I don't want to walk up five floors. Let's
   take the _____ .

5 Do you ever buy things from online _____ ?
   You can get some real bargains.

6 Katie doesn't _____ a house – she lives
   with her parents.

7 It's expensive to buy _____ space in a
   magazine.

8 I _____ my old computer up for sale but
   no one bought it.

4 Match words 1–6 with photos A–F.

1 [A] saucer   4 [ ] stall
2 [ ] craft   5 [ ] crossing
3 [ ] antique   6 [ ] cube

LOOK RIGHT →

A   B   C   D   E   F

5 Complete the sentences with the correct adjectives.

> colourful ~~crowded~~ enormous tasty trendy

1 There were lots of people in the department
   store – it was really *crowded* .

2 The street market is two kilometres long – it's
   _____ !

3 I love that _____ new café – it's so cool!

4 The meal was very _____ – you're a great cook.

5 Your dress is so _____ – it's like a rainbow!

6 Complete the email with words from this page.

From: Gemma;
To: Trisha;

Hi Trisha,
I had a brilliant time in London last weekend! On the first
day, we went to an ¹*enormous* street market with hundreds
of ² _____ selling clothes, toys and crafts. Mum wanted
something new for the breakfast table and she bought some
pretty cups and ³ _____ . Lots of hipsters go to the market,
so it's a really ⁴ _____ place to visit.

As you know, dad collects ⁵ _____ toys – he has lots of toy
soldiers from the 1930s! So the next day, we went to an
⁶ _____ where people were buying and selling vintage toys.
It was really ⁷ _____ as there were hundreds of people there.
Dad was really happy!

What did you do at the weekend? Did you have fun?
Gemma

7 Read the video script. Underline any words or phrases you don't know and find their meaning in your dictionary.

City shopping

Part 1

We buy a lot of things online but we also like to go to shops. And when you're on holiday in a big city, it's exciting to see the famous shopping areas. Every big city has its own special places to shop. Think about London, Paris, New York and Tokyo.
5 What shops do you imagine? Let's look at some of the most famous shopping areas in the world.

Oxford Street in London is the busiest shopping street in Europe. It has around three hundred shops and half a million people visit it every day. In Oxford Street you can find enormous department stores and buy both expensive and cheap things. You
10 probably know the names. There's Marks and Spencer, Primark, Forever 21, Gap, H&M, and of course, the first department store, Selfridges. It's a wonderful shop to visit. The best time to go to Oxford Street is at Christmas. The lights are very special. Every year, in November, a celebrity switches the lights on. Lots of people go to watch this. It's usually a famous singer or sports star. Oxford Street is always very
15 crowded. Sometimes it's difficult to move along the pavements! The traffic is very bad too. Cars and buses make a lot of pollution.

Another popular shopping area in London is Portobello Road and it's very different. Here you can find lots of small shops that sell trendy things. On Saturdays there is an enormous market with more than 1,000 stalls! They sell everything. You can
20 buy amazing, exotic food to eat – cheap, hot and tasty. There are also stalls that sell unusual crafts, like pretty cups and saucers, and pictures by local artists. Or you can look for antiques. Some people say it's the biggest antiques market in the world. And if you like vintage clothes and accessories, this is the place to go. Tourists love to come here and walk along nearly two kilometres of market.

25 ## Part 2

Do you know the most expensive shopping street in the world? At the moment, it's Fifth Avenue in New York. Here you can find expensive jewellery in Tiffany's, expensive handbags in Louis Vuitton, and expensive clothes in Gucci and Prada. The world-famous Apple Store is a wonderful glass cube. People come here to buy
30 phones and tablets but they also come just to take photographs.

Also in New York, there is another important store to visit. This is Macy's. It's called the largest store in the world. Some people don't agree with this but it's definitely the biggest store in the USA. It sells lots of different things and it's a really interesting shop to go to. It's very big and you need to walk a lot to see it all.

35 Let's cross the world to Tokyo. Here we can find another very famous shopping area: Shibuya. And it has perhaps the most famous street crossing in the world! At Shibuya Crossing when the traffic lights go red, they stop all the cars. People cross the roads quickly at the same time. It's amazing. Near the crossing are very big neon advertisements and huge video screens. It's a busy, bright and colourful
40 place. The Shibuya shopping area is very popular with young trendy people. It's full of shops, game stores, restaurants and clubs. This is where you can see new Japanese fashion and have a lot of fun!

Learning to work

I can talk about people and their jobs.

1 ● Match jobs 1–8 with photos A–H.

1	*E* builder	5	☐	firefighter
2	☐ artist	6	☐	pilot
3	☐ hairdresser	7	☐	lawyer
4	☐ mechanic	8	☐	nurse

2 ● Match words 1–5 with words a–e to make jobs.

1	*e* police	a	guide
2	☐ tour	b	assistant
3	☐ IT	c	courier
4	☐ bike	d	specialist
5	☐ sales	e	officer

3 ●● Which jobs are the people talking about?

1 People come to me when they arrive at the hotel. I'm a(n) *receptionist*.
2 I design new buildings. I'm a(n) _____.
3 I fix cars. I'm a(n) _____.
4 I write stories for newspapers. I'm a(n) _____.
5 I paint pictures. I'm a(n) _____.
6 I work outside and I keep cows and pigs. I'm a(n) _____.
7 I cook meals for people in my restaurant. I'm a(n) _____.
8 I fly planes and helicopters. I'm a(n) _____.

4 ⚫⚫ Complete the sentences with the correct words.

> farmer   police officer   ~~builder~~   electrician
> gardener   pilot   tour guide   postman
> soldier   waiter

1 My uncle is a(n) _builder_ and he helped my dad put up a wall in our garden.
2 The _____ was late this morning so I didn't get the letter until two o'clock.
3 There's a problem with the lights in my bedroom. We need a(n) _____.
4 I've got a summer job as a(n) _____ in a café in town. I serve customers coffee and sandwiches.
5 It takes a long time to become a(n) _____ and fly planes.
6 Someone stole my dad's car and a(n) _____ came to our house today to ask questions.
7 I'd like to be a(n) _____ and show tourists around interesting places and historic buildings.
8 A(n) _____ has a hard life. They get up really early to feed their animals.
9 My brother is in the army. He's a(n) _____.
10 I want to be a(n) _____ because I can work outside and grow flowers and plants.

5 ⚫⚫ WORD FRIENDS Order the words to make questions or sentences.

1 to / people / from / five / work / nine / some
Some people work from nine to five.
2 you / work / happy / at / are / ?
_____
3 don't / indoors / work / farmers
_____
4 wouldn't / uniform / like / a / I / wear / to
_____
5 get / on / must / time / work / you / to
_____
6 to / team / a / need / in / work / firefighters
_____
7 do / have / teachers / weekend / the / at / work / to / ?
_____
8 work / secretaries / indoors / usually
_____
9 often / work / have / drivers / early / start / bus / to
_____

6 ⚫⚫ Complete the sentences with the correct words.

> happy   team   earn   ~~wear~~   time   from
> alone   weekend

1 Firefighters have to _wear_ a uniform at work.
2 Most sales assistants work _____ nine to five.
3 Artists usually work _____.
4 I think it's important to be _____ at work.
5 Lawyers can _____ good money.
6 I need to get up early to get to work on _____.
7 My dad's a doctor and he often has to work at the _____.
8 In a hospital nurses have to work in a _____.

7 ⚫⚫⚫ Complete the text with the correct words.

I'm still a student but I have a part time [1]job. I'm a [2]_____ at a restaurant in my town. I take the meals from the kitchen to the customers. I like my job. I don't earn much [3]_____ but it's fun. It's nice to work [4]_____ a team and I like the [5]_____ a lot. He cooks great food! I have to work at the [6]_____ so I can't go out a lot with my friends on Saturdays and Sundays. I also have to wear a blue and white [7]_____ but that's OK! In the future I'd like to be a [8]_____ like my dad and work for a newspaper or an [9]_____ like my mum, and design houses. I think it's important to work when you're a student. You learn lots of things, like – it's important to [10]_____ to work on time. Also it's important to be happy [11]_____ work. I'm happy in my job now and I hope I can be happy in the future too.

I can use *will* to talk about future predictions.

1 Complete the sentences with the correct words.

> timetable   classroom   uniform   ~~break~~
> course book   test

1 We usually have a *break* at 11.30 and we can go outside for half an hour.
2 A: Which room is Geography in?
   B: I don't know – look at the _____.
3 This _____ is good. The pictures are interesting and the exercises are too.
4 I quite like our school _____. The colours are nice.
5 We're having a French _____ today and I can't remember anything!
6 I left my phone in the _____. Wait for me.

2 ● Complete the sentences with *will* and the correct verbs.

> rain   be   work   win   ~~get~~   break

1 Helena *will get* the best marks in the test. She's very clever.
2 It _____ at the weekend. I heard that on the radio.
3 In 2020 I _____ a teacher and I'll live in the countryside.
4 Be careful! You _____ the pen!
5 Our team is very good. I think they _____ the match.
6 People _____ from their homes in the future.

3 ● Make negative sentences and questions from the positive predictions.

1 Danny will pass the exam.
   N: *Danny won't pass the exam.*
   Q: *Will Danny pass the exam?*
2 It will rain tomorrow.
   N: _____
   Q: _____
3 Prices will be lower in the summer.
   N: _____
   Q: _____
4 In the future children will start school at the age of three.
   N: _____
   Q: _____

4 ●● Make predictions with *will/won't*.

1 Wait here. I / not / be / long
   I won't be long.
2 you / help me / with this homework / later / ?
   _____
3 The journey is short; It / only / take / an hour
   _____
4 I / not think / Miss Jones / teach us / next term
   _____
5 where / your family live / in England / ?
   _____
6 people / live longer / in the future
   _____

5 ●●● Complete the text with the correct future form of the verbs in brackets.

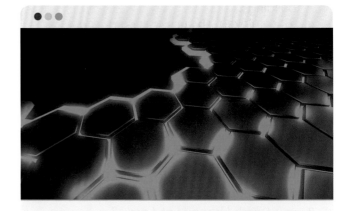

So, what [1] *will shopping be* (shopping/be) like in the future? No one knows definitely but I think we [2]_____ (do) ALL our shopping online. People [3]_____ (not need) to go out to shops. For food – our fridge [4]_____ (tell) our computers what we need. We [5]_____ (not have to) do anything! Robots [6]_____ (drive) the food to our houses and put it directly into our fridges and cupboards. But [7]_____ (robots/choose) our clothes too? No, I don't think they [8]_____. We [9]_____ (go) online, choose our clothes and then we [10]_____ (see) a picture of ourselves in the jeans or dress on our screens and we [11]_____ (decide) to buy or not to buy! Of course, we [12]_____ (not have) any money in our wallets in the future. We [13]_____ (pay) for everything automatically. So, in the future there [14]_____ (not be) any sales assistants or bankers, just lots of IT specialists and robots.

I can find specific detail in a text and talk about children's dreams and ambitions.

1 Complete the sentences with the correct words.

> full-time   part-time   ~~temporary~~   summer

1 My friend has a *temporary* job in the supermarket for the next six weeks but then he'll need to find another one.
2 My mum did a _____ job while I was very young. She only worked a few hours every day.
3 I want to get a _____ job during July and August before I go to college.
4 My dad works from nine to five at the bank. It's a _____ job. This is his tenth year there!

2 Choose the correct answers.

1 A secretary usually works _____ an office.
  a on   b at   ⓒ in
2 If you're looking _____ a job, let me know.
  a for   b over   c on
3 At the moment I'm _____ but I think I'll find a job soon.
  a employed   b unemployed   c employing
4 My brother worked _____ a waiter last summer and earned a lot of money.
  a like   b by   c as
5 Jake _____ his job in the supermarket because he never got there on time.
  a got   b lost   c missed
6 My granddad worked _____ the same company for fifty years!
  a about   b for   c into

3 Read the text. Mark the sentences ✓ (right), ✗ (wrong) or ? (doesn't say).

1 [✓] The writer believes that children often want to have the same job as famous people or people they know.
2 [ ] The writer wanted to be on television.
3 [ ] The writer works on television now.
4 [ ] Boys and girls have different types of dream jobs.
5 [ ] Today's children will earn more than their parents did.
6 [ ] It isn't a good idea to have an unrealistic dream.
7 [ ] The writer thinks that people's dreams stay the same through their lives.

4 Complete the sentences with the correct words.

> ambitious   ~~admired~~   realistic
> princesses   definite   survey

1 When I was young I *admired* my cousin who was a police officer because he seemed so strong.
2 If I'm _____, I don't think I'll ever be very rich.
3 Let's answer the questions in this _____. It looks interesting.
4 My brother isn't very _____. He just wants an easy job.
5 It will be sunny tomorrow. That's _____!
6 Some _____ work very hard these days.

What was your dream?

What were your dreams and ambitions when you were a child? Are your dreams the same now? Nearly all children have a dream for the future. Sometimes they want to be like people they see on television or someone in their family. When I was a child I wanted to be a lawyer because I admired the lawyer in a TV drama! My sister wanted to be a princess!

A recent survey asked 11,000 seven-year-olds about their ambitions and the results were interesting. Most of them had definite ideas about their future careers. The most popular jobs included teacher, scientist, firefighter and police officer. In general boys wanted to earn a lot of money (a third of them wanted to become a footballer or sportsman) and girls preferred a job helping people, like a doctor or teacher.

Experts say that today's children have greater ambitions than their parents had and this is a very good thing. People who have a dream will work harder and have fewer problems. Sometimes those dreams aren't realistic and they change. Not every seven-year-old boy will become a rich and successful footballer! I didn't become a lawyer – and surprisingly, my sister didn't become a princess! But it is important to be ambitious. We all need to dream.

I can use the First Conditional to talk about probability.

1 **WORD FRIENDS** **Choose the correct option.**

1 I must *learn* / (*revise*) for my English test tomorrow.

2 Unfortunately I *missed* / *failed* my Maths test yesterday because I didn't study.

3 We're going to *write* / *take* a test next week in History.

4 We're *getting* / *finding* the results of our tests on Thursday next week.

5 I never *make* / *get* a good mark in end of term tests. I get too nervous.

6 The teacher sent Harry home because he *cheated* / *failed* in a test.

2 ● **Put *if* in the correct position in the sentences. Add commas where necessary.**

1 ⟨If⟩ dad doesn't arrive home soon ⟨,⟩ his dinner will be cold.

2 ⟨x⟩ We won't fail our tests ⟨if⟩ we work hard.

3 ☐ I'll be happy ☐ I get a good mark.

4 ☐ I get home too late ☐ I won't call you.

5 ☐ I won't go running ☐ it's very cold and rainy.

6 ☐ I get a summer job ☐ I'll earn lots of money.

7 ☐ you don't go to bed soon ☐ you'll be very tired tomorrow.

3 ●● **Match the parts of the sentences.**

1 ⟨g⟩ If the bus is late,

2 ☐ If my dad doesn't like his new job,

3 ☐ If I don't see you after school,

4 ☐ If we get good marks,

5 ☐ If the jeans don't fit,

6 ☐ If we win the game on Saturday,

7 ☐ If you don't work hard,

a I'll take them back to the shop tomorrow.

b we'll be the best team in town.

c you won't get a good job.

d I'll see you at the party.

e our teacher will be really pleased.

f he'll find a different one.

g I'll miss the start of the film.

4 ●● **Complete the sentences with the correct form of the verbs in brackets.**

1 If dad **drives** (drive) us to the cinema, we **'ll get** (get) there by 4.30.

2 I _____ (not buy) any tickets if you _____ (not want) to go to the concert.

3 We _____ (be) back home before lunch if we _____ (leave) now.

4 If you _____ (go) to France in May, you _____ (have) sunny weather.

5 David _____ (have to) wear a uniform if he _____ (become) a police officer.

6 If the teacher _____ (not give) us a test tomorrow, I _____ (be) very happy.

7 _____ (you/wait) for me if my train _____ (be) late?

5 ●●● **Complete the dialogue with the correct form of the verbs.**

> buy   not see   ~~miss~~   not have
> go   ask   be   give   spend

A: The new clothes shop has a sale on today! Let's go after school.

B: I've got a swimming lesson after school. If I [1]*miss* it, my teacher will be angry.

A: But if I [2]_____ without you and get some cheap boots, you [3]_____ angry!

B: If you [4]_____ any more money you [5]_____ enough to go on holiday!

A: Ah. It's my birthday soon. If I [6]_____ my parents, they [7]_____ me money instead of a present.

B: OK! But I can't miss swimming. If I give you some money, [8]_____ me a cheap black T-shirt?

A: Yeah. If I [9]_____ any cheap ones, I'll buy you something else.

B: No, don't! Don't buy anything then!

I can identify specific detail in a conversation and talk about education.

1 Choose the odd one out.

1 primary school   (Maths teacher)
   secondary school   university
2 head teacher   classmate   staff room
   form tutor
3 science laboratory   classroom   library   pupil
4 sports field   gymnasium   playground
   cloakroom

2 Use the clues to complete the crossword. What is number 10?

```
¹c  o  l  l  ¹⁰e  g  e
         2
              3
      4
         5
   6
      7
      8
9
```

1 You study here when you finish secondary school.
2 The teacher who is in charge of your school is a … teacher.
3 A young person who goes to school.
4 You study this subject in a laboratory.
5 You can borrow books from here.
6 A student who is in your class.
7 You do indoor sports here.
8 A room at school where you can leave your coat.
9 An outdoor area for children to play.

3 WORD FRIENDS Complete the sentences with the correct words.

| do ×2   give   ~~make~~   write

1 Did you *make* any notes in our History lesson today?
2 We have to _____ a long essay for English tonight.
3 If we _____ Exercises 1 and 2 now, we won't need to _____ any homework tonight!
4 Tomorrow Jason is going to _____ a presentation about New York in class.

4 🔊 18 Listen to the radio phone in and choose the correct answers.

1 Where does the interviewer think his listeners are?

A   B   C

2 Where does Monica usually have her lessons?

A   B   C

3 How does Monica's mum know what to teach?

A   B   C

4 Why is Monica not studying at school?

A   B   C

5 What would Monica sometimes like to do?

A   B   C

I can talk about probability.

1 Order the words to make sentences.

a to / will / early / definitely / I / tonight / go / bed   *I will definitely go to bed early tonight.*

b tomorrow / go / shopping / might / I   _____

c won't / horror / definitely / the / I / film / watch   _____

d probably / today / this / finish / won't / essay / I   _____

e will / friends / some / email / this / probably / evening / I   _____

2 Order the sentences from Exercise 1 (1 = most certain to happen, 5 = least certain to happen).

1 [a]   2 [ ]   3 [ ]   4 [ ]   5 [ ]

3 Write sentences about pictures 1–7.

Key
✓✓ – will definitely
?✓ – will probably
?   – may/might
?✗ – probably won't
✗✗ – definitely won't

1 *I'll definitely learn to play the guitar.*

2 _____

3 _____

4 _____

5 _____

6 _____

7 _____

4 🔊 19 Match gaps 1–6 with sentences a–f. Then listen and check.

A: Hi Beth! The Rubies are playing in town tonight at the Grange Theatre. Mike and I are going. ¹e

B: Oh, I'm not sure. ²___ If I finish early, I'll come.

A: Oh, Beth. The Rubies are more important than work. ³___ I know! I can help you with your work.

B: Brilliant! ⁴___ What time are you and Mike going?

A: ⁵___ I'm going to phone him in a moment to confirm. Do you want to meet us there?

B: ⁶___ I only get home from swimming at 7.20. How about I meet you inside at 7.45?

A: OK. Let me help you with that work now!

a I definitely won't be there by 7.30.

b I might come but I've got a lot of work.

c We'll probably meet outside the Grange about 7.30.

d They probably won't come to our town again for a long time.

e Would you like to come too?

f Then I'll definitely come!

I can talk about people's skills and emotions.

1 Complete the sentences with the correct prepositions. Then match sentences 1–9 with pictures A–I.

> in at of about on

1 I'm good *at* French.
2 I'm keen _____ sports.
3 I'm interested _____ languages.
4 I'm afraid _____ the dark.
5 I'm brilliant _____ History.
6 I'm fond _____ my young sister.
7 I'm hopeless _____ Maths.
8 I'm crazy _____ pop music.
9 I'm bad _____ Art.

A

B

C

D

E

F

G

H

I

2 Match sentences 1–9 in Exercise 1 with sentences a–i below.

a ☐ I speak Russian, Swedish and Italian.
b ☐ I can't draw or paint.
c ☐ I always leave the light on at night.
d ☐ I listen to it all the time.
e ☐ I can remember dates of important events very easily.
f ☐ 1 ☐ I practise every year when we go to Paris on holiday.
g ☐ I look after her when my parents go out.
h ☐ I play football, tennis and basketball.
i ☐ I always ask my friend to help me prepare for tests.

3 Read the sentences about Katy's ambitions. Choose the correct answers.

1 I'm really _____ of animals. I'd like to be a vet.
 a brilliant ⓑ fond c keen
2 It won't be easy because I'm hopeless _____ Maths and Science at the moment!
 a at b in c of
3 I'm interested in _____ all about the different types of animals.
 a to learn b learn c learning
4 I enjoy _____ my friends' dogs for a walk.
 a to take b take c taking
5 I'm not _____ of working hard.
 a afraid b hopeless c bad
6 When I was young I was crazy about _____ animal books and magazines.
 a to read b read c reading
7 Then I got very keen _____ taking our neighbour's dog for walks.
 a about b on c at
8 I'm quite _____ at understanding how animals feel.
 a good b keen c fond
9 It _____ good to work with animals all the time.
 a will be b definitely be c are

For each learning objective, tick (✓) the box that best matches your ability.

☺☺ = I understand and can help a friend.

☺ = I understand and can do it by myself.

☹ = I understand but have some questions.

☹☹ = I do not understand.

		☺☺	☺	☹	☹☹	Need help?	Now try ...
8.1	Vocabulary					Students' Book pp. 94–95 Workbook pp. 90–91	Ex. 1–3, p. 99
8.2	Grammar					Students' Book p. 96 Workbook p. 92	Ex. 4–5, p. 99
8.3	Reading					Students' Book p. 97 Workbook p. 93	
8.4	Grammar					Students' Book p. 98 Workbook p. 94	
8.5	Listening					Students' Book p. 99 Workbook p. 95	
8.6	Speaking					Students' Book p. 100 Workbook p. 96	Ex. 6, p. 99
8.7	English in Use					Students' Book p. 101 Workbook p. 97	

8.1   I can talk about people and their jobs.

8.2   I can use *will* to talk about future predictions.

8.3   I can find specific detail in a text and talk about children's dreams and ambitions.

8.4   I can use the First Conditional to talk about probability.

8.5   I can identify specific detail in a conversation and talk about education.

8.6   I can talk about probability.

8.7   I can talk about people's skills and emotions.

What can you remember from this unit?

New words I learned (the words you most want to remember from this unit)	**Expressions and phrases I liked** (any expressions or phrases you think sound nice, useful or funny)	**English I heard or read outside class** (e.g. from websites, books, adverts, films, music)

Vocabulary

1 Complete the sentences with the correct jobs.

1 My dad is a _____ and he writes articles for magazines and newspapers.
2 My friend loves repairing cars and motorbikes and he wants to be a _____ .
3 I don't want to be an _____ like my cousin. He just calculates numbers for businesses all day.
4 All our lights went off this morning. We need an _____ to fix the problem.
5 My brother is training to be an _____ . He wants to design modern, eco-friendly buildings.
6 The police arrested Kevin for dangerous driving. He needs a good _____ or he'll go to prison.

2 Choose the correct option.

1 Some people don't want to work *in* / *for* a company so they start their own business.
2 It's important to work *at* / *in* a team if you want to get results.
3 After university my brother worked *as* / *like* a postman for two months.
4 Nelson is hopeless *in* / *at* getting to work on time.
5 It's great to *win* / *earn* a lot of money but it's more important to be happy at work.
6 When the company closed, a lot of people *were* / *had* unemployed.
7 I'm really interested *for* / *in* learning more about jobs like this.
8 Richard is looking *at* / *for* a summer job this year.

3 Complete the sentences with the correct words.

classmates   head   library
playground   pupils   staff

1 My primary school was very small and it only had sixty _____ .
2 I'd like to speak to Miss Turner. Is she in the _____ room?
3 The class teacher sent Tom to see the _____ teacher because he was fighting in class.
4 At break all the children play games in the _____ .
5 Let's work in the _____ . It's quieter there than in the class.
6 I get on well with all my _____ . We're good friends.

Grammar

4 Complete the sentences with *will* and the verbs below.

be x2   be able   not be   not finish
not get   go   phone   stay   watch

1 In the future there _____ any TVs. We _____ films and programmes on computers.
2 _____ (you) at a hotel in Spain on holiday next week?
3 After university I _____ a job immediately. I _____ travelling for a few months.
4 Jan _____ seventeen next Sunday. She _____ to learn to drive!
5 _____ (you) at home this evening? I _____ you at about 7.30.
6 The test tomorrow _____ before 12.15.

5 Choose the correct option.

1 *Does* / *Will* your brother take his driving test again if he *fails* / *will fail* it tomorrow?
2 If I *go* / *will go* to bed late tonight, I *am* / *will be* tired tomorrow.
3 We *move* / *will move* to the USA if my dad *gets* / *will get* a new job.
4 Where *do you* / *will you* swim if they *close* / *will close* the Sports Centre?
5 If I *don't* / *won't* get good results, my parents *aren't* / *won't be* happy!

Speaking language practice

6 Order the words to make sentences or questions.

1 Look at the time! be / will / late / definitely / we _____
2 probably / you / won't / I / see / later _____ Good luck with the exam!
3 Don't leave. arrive / they / soon / might _____
4 you / party / come / the / definitely / to / will / ? _____ It will be great!
5 Sophie doesn't eat a lot. might / meal / want / big / she / a / not _____
6 Take an umbrella. rain / it / later / may _____

Unit 8 **99**

1 Match jobs 1–8 with photos A–H.

1 [B] travel agent   5 ☐ pharmacist
2 ☐ librarian   6 ☐ bar tender
3 ☐ care worker   7 ☐ secretary
4 ☐ check-in   8 ☐ soldier
     assistant

2 Complete the sentences with the correct form of the verbs.

check   code   look   ~~progress~~
manufacture   replace

1 My English is definitely *progressing* – I can understand a lot more now.
2 Last year, we _____ our old PC with a fast new laptop.
3 I didn't learn to _____ at school but my younger sister did.
4 They _____ these cars in Germany.
5 A really nice doctor _____ after my sister when she was in hospital.
6 We don't need to _____ in to the hotel before twelve o'clock.

3 Look at photos A–F. In which photo …

1 [C] is a robot protecting the door?
2 ☐ is a robot welcoming visitors?
3 ☐ is a receptionist speaking Japanese?
4 ☐ is a receptionist speaking bad English?
5 ☐ is a robot carrying visitors' bags?
6 ☐ is a robot going to turn off the lights?

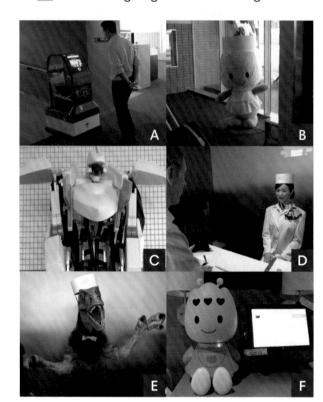

4 Match verbs 1–4 with words and phrases a–d to make Word Friends.

1 [e] make   a energy
2 ☐ give   b orders
3 ☐ save   c a uniform
4 ☐ wear   d somebody laugh

5 Complete the sentences with the correct form of the Word Friends from Exercise 4.

1 We switch off the lights to *save energy*.
2 A boss usually _____ to his workers.
3 He _____ us _____ with his funny jokes.
4 I _____ – a red jumper and a grey skirt.

6 Choose the correct option.

1 My mum loves working as a (librarian)/ care worker because she enjoys reading.
2 Do they use facial *recognition* / *understanding* at airports?
3 Please *turn off* / *save* the lights when you go.
4 We don't go to a *check-in assistant* / *travel agent* – we book our holidays online.

7 Read the video script. Underline any words or phrases you don't know and find their meaning in your dictionary.

The amazing Henn Na Hotel

Part 1

Tourists in Japan usually go to see traditional Japanese buildings but there is a new tourist attraction and it's a very modern and unusual building.

Welcome to the Henn Na Hotel – it's a new hotel and a very unusual one. A

5 tall robot protects the door and then a pink doll robot welcomes visitors when they come in. She's very friendly. There are two receptionists. The big question is – do they speak English?

"Kon'nichi wa. Do you speak English?"

The first receptionist is a woman with dark hair. She's wearing a smart uniform.

10 She's pretty and she's smiling but … she's a robot too. And, no, she doesn't speak English.

So our visitor goes to the second receptionist. He's surprised! This receptionist is … a dinosaur! The visitor pushes a button and he starts to speak.

"Welcome. Welcome to the Henn Na Hotel."

15 It's English but it isn't very good unfortunately and it's quite funny.

"Thank you for your visitors."

He makes the visitor laugh. "On top of the filling the phone number, please put us to the bottom of the post. Please press to proceed with the send too."

He welcomes the visitor and tells him what he needs to do. "Please move to

20 the right hand panel and check in." First, he must go to another machine.

It takes a photograph of his face.

The hotel rooms don't have keys and the doors use facial recognition.

"Thank you so much." Now our visitor knows his room number. What other surprises are waiting for him at this amazing hotel?

25 ## Part 2

Here at the Henn Na Hotel, you don't need to carry your bags. A machine, not a person, carries them for you. It's called a 'portabot' and it's clever but … very slow. In English the name 'henn na' means 'strange' – and it really is! Here there are only robots and machines, no people!

30 Finally, at the room, the visitor stands in front of the door and … the door opens. It knows him because of the photograph from the machine in reception.

Inside the room everything is automatic. They want to save energy at the hotel. There are no light switches because visitors usually forget to turn

35 them off. There's a computer you can use. And of course there's also a speaking robot. She's called Churi Chan. You can ask her questions and give her orders. The problem is that she only speaks Japanese, so there's a book with translations.

Our visitor asks: 'What time is it now'? and 'How is the weather today?' and

40 she tells him. Then he tells her to switch off the lights. She does. But then he has a problem – it's too dark to read the instructions to turn the lights back on again.

I can talk about landscapes, natural features and countries.

Close to nature

VOCABULARY
Landscapes and natural features |
Phrasal verbs | Outdoor activities |
Sporting equipment

GRAMMAR
Present Perfect – all forms | Present
Perfect with *just/already/yet*

READING
A blog about a survival story |
Multiple choice

LISTENING
Matching people and sports

SPEAKING
Asking for, giving and
refusing permission

WRITING
A postcard

B B C CULTURE
How many fish ... ?

EXAM TIME 3 > p. 122

1 ● Look at photos 1–8 and complete the names for natural features.

1 b*each*
2 c _ _ _ _
3 l _ _ _ _
4 r _ _ _ _ _
5 f _ _ _ _ _
6 i _ _ _ _ _
7 r _ _ _ _ _
8 s _ _

2 ●● Use the clues to complete the crossword.

Across
3 an area of land with lots
  of tropical plants and trees
4 a forest with tall trees,
  warm climate and lots
  of rain
6 very big sea
8 where a river falls over
  a cliff
9 hot and dry area with
  no plants

Down
1 very high hill
2 a hill with a hole at the top
  that sometimes has fire
  coming from it
5 an area of grass where
  farmers can grow things
7 this is where the land
  meets the sea

3 ●● Read the notices. Then complete the labels with the correct words.

> a cliff   a desert   a beach
> ~~a mountain~~   rainforest
> a river   a field

1 Check the weather forecast before starting to climb.

a mountain

2 Use the bridge to cross – 300 metres away.

3 No water for the next 50 km.

4 Sun chairs here   50p an hour

5 NO CLIMBING. DANGER – FALLING ROCKS.

6 Help the environment – save the trees!

7 Public path but please shut the gate – farm animals.

4 ●● Match notices 1–7 from Exercise 3 with meanings a–g below.

a ☐ You can walk across here, but be careful.

b ☐ You don't have to lie on the sand.

c ☐ You mustn't do this – it's dangerous.

d ☐1☐ Weather change can make this place dangerous.

e ☐ We need to think about the future.

f ☐ Take something to drink with you.

g ☐ You need to walk a short way to find something.

5 ● WORD FRIENDS Choose the correct option.

1 We went skiing ⟨in⟩/ on the mountains last year.

2 We saw some black cows on / in a big field.

3 My uncle has a house by / on a lake.

4 My parents would like to live in / on the coast so they can look at the sea every day.

5 My friend lives in / on an island and has to take a boat to go to school every morning.

6 We can walk along this path and then have a picnic by / in the river.

6 ●● Choose the correct answers.

1 I live about 100 kilometres from England's ___ city, London.
   a official   ⓑ capital   c national

2 I live with my parents in a small house on the south ___ .
   a beach   b sea   c coast

3 Our house is in a village where the ___ is only 540!
   a population   b country   c border

4 It takes five minutes to get to the ___ and we often go swimming there in summer.
   a cliff   b island   c beach

5 From the window of my room I can see the farmer's ___ with black and white cows.
   a fields   b rocks   c waterfall

6 I can cycle along a path to a ___ where we sometimes pick flowers and mushrooms.
   a jungle   b forest   c desert

7 I love living here in the countryside because of all the lovely ___ features.
   a natural   b capital   c country

7 ●● Choose the correct option.

If you're looking for somewhere to spend a holiday that is full of lovely natural ¹borders / ⟨features⟩, then come to the New Forest! It is one of the most beautiful areas in the ²capital / country. If you stay in a hotel in a New Forest village, you can go on trips to the ³coast / rocks and visit such beautiful cities as Winchester and Salisbury. If you like walking, then the New Forest is the place for you! You can look at different types of trees, follow small ⁴lakes / rivers and see the famous New Forest horses. They are free to walk anywhere, even on the roads, and don't live in ⁵islands / fields. If you go to the ⁶rainforest / sea, you can walk along the ⁷beaches / jungle and look across the water to some pretty ⁸flags / islands. The ⁹cliffs / desert along the beaches are high and can be dangerous so don't walk too close to them. Interested in the New Forest? Check out our website …

I can use the Present Perfect to talk about experience.

1 ● Complete the sentences with the positive Present Perfect form of the verbs.

| eat   win   ~~sleep~~   write   play   see

1 I *have slept* in a tent.
2 My brother _____ two short stories.
3 My mother _____ Mexican food.
4 My cousins _____ basketball in the USA.
5 You _____ lots of medals.
6 Danny _____ the Eiffel Tower.

2 ●● Order the words to make sentences or questions.

1 been / Italy / I've / to / never
I've never been to Italy.
2 you / rabbit / ever / eaten / have / ?
_____
3 never / to / our teacher / forgotten / mark / homework / has / our
_____
4 seen / we / new / film / the / horror / haven't
_____
5 never / my / played / has / football / brother
_____
6 computer / crashed / has / ever / your / ?
_____
7 times / how / been / have / France / you / many / to / ?
_____

3 ●● Make sentences or questions in the Present Perfect.

1 you / ever / meet / someone famous / ?
Have you ever met someone famous?
2 I / never / fly / in a helicopter
_____
3 Erin / not / see / the new TV talent show
_____
4 how many people / you / invite / to your party / ?
_____
5 we / not / study / the Present Perfect before
_____
6 your parents / ever / live / in another country / ?
_____
7 which countries / in Europe / you / visit / ?
_____
8 my friends / never / eat / Chinese food
_____

4 ●●● Complete the dialogue with the correct form of the verbs in brackets.

A: So, you'd like to be a tour guide for our company. [1]*Have you been* (you/be) to many countries?

B: Yes. I [2]_____ (travel) a lot. I [3]_____ (be) to most European countries on holiday and I [4]_____ (stay) with friends in the USA twice.

A: [5]_____ (you/ever/give) talks or presentations about famous sights?

B: Yes, [6]_____ (do) quite a lot! At school! I'm really interested in museums and important buildings. I [7]_____ (also/do) some projects about famous art galleries in the world.

A: Excellent. What other experience do you have that's important for a tour guide?

B: Well, I [8]_____ (learn) three languages and passed exams in all three. So I now speak French, Chinese and Russian. I think that will help.

A: Oh, yes.

B: And I [9]_____ (make) lots of friends in different countries so I know quite a lot about different cultures.

A: Very good. I think you'll be very good for the job!

I can find specific detail in a text and talk about personal adventures.

1 Choose the correct answers.

1 I know you're tired but don't give _____ . Keep running!

   a on   (b) up   c over

2 When did this event _____ place?

   a take   b make   c do

3 Have you come _____ my dictionary? I left it in here.

   a over   b at   c across

4 The bomb hit the building and it blew _____ .

   a off   b up   c down

5 I need to find _____ when the film starts.

   a in   b out   c up

2 Read the blog and choose the correct answers.

1 Joe Simpson and Simon Yates

   a were from Peru.

   b met while they were climbing Siula Grande.

   (c) had the same ambition.

2 Because of the bad weather

   a they didn't get to the top of the mountain.

   b Joe had an accident.

   c Simon lost the rope.

3 On the way down the mountain Simon

   a saved Joe's life.

   b saved his own life.

   c died.

4 After Joe fell into the hole

   a he climbed back up again.

   b he found his way home.

   c he stayed there for three days.

5 Since 1985 Joe

   a has published some books.

   b has never climbed again.

   c has made a film about his survival.

3 Write the correct word from the text for each definition.

1 A person who climbs mountains: *mountaineer*

2 A person you work with or do sports with: _____

3 Someone who lives through something dangerous: _____

4 Something we pull or hold on to: _____

5 Doctors do this to make us better: _____

6 A person who makes a film: _____

My blog

ABOUT ME   **MY POSTS**   CONTACT ME

I've seen quite a lot of films about survivors but my favourite is a true story about an English mountaineer called Joe Simpson. He climbed a very dangerous mountain, Siula Grande in Peru, in 1985 with his friend and partner Simon Yates. Joe and Simon wanted to be the first people to climb the West Face of the mountain.

When they started the weather was fine but then it changed. The two climbers reached the top successfully but then they had to get back down quickly because of the bad weather. Unfortunately Joe then fell and broke his leg. Simon tried to help his friend get down the mountain. He tied him onto a long rope but the weather got worse and he had to make a terrible decision. He had to cut the rope that was holding Joe or die.

Simon cut the rope and Joe fell into a big hole. Luckily Joe found a way out of the hole at the bottom. It took him three days to get down the rest of the mountain. With his broken leg he could only move very slowly. He had no food or water and when he got to the camp he was nearly dead. But he got there and he lived!

Joe wrote a book called 'Touching the Void' about the experience and in 2003 director Kevin MacDonald made a film with the same title. Since his adventure Joe has had lots of operations on his leg. Doctors told him never to climb again. But he has! He has also written several books and given lots of presentations about climbing. In my opinion 'Touching the Void' is the best film about survival that I've ever seen.

[leave a comment]

I can use the Present Perfect to talk about recent events.

1 ● Put the words in brackets in the correct position in the sentences.

1 I've woken up. (just)
I've just woken up.

2 I've read that book. (already)
_____

3 We haven't studied the grammar. (yet)
_____

4 Mick has phoned. (just)
_____

5 Has the teacher marked our homework? (yet)
_____

6 I haven't been to the beach. (yet)
_____

2 ●● Match the sentences in Exercise 1 with sentences a–f below.

a ☐ He can't go swimming with us.
b 1 I'm really tired.
c ☐ Is it sandy?
d ☐ Have you got another one?
e ☐ We gave it to her a week ago.
f ☐ We can't do this exercise.

3 ●● Order the words to make sentences or questions.

1 the / yet / been / exhibition / have / new / to / you / ?
Have you been to the new exhibition yet?

2 just / Spain / dad / in / holiday / booked / has / our
_____
_____

3 spoken / about / I / the / yet / haven't / to / concert / Bill
_____
_____

4 seen / we've / film / that / already
_____

5 just / your / I've / email / opened
_____

6 party / she / the / invited / to / already / you / has / ?
_____
_____

4 ●● Rewrite the sentences using *already*, *just* or *yet*.

1 I spoke to Pat a few moments ago.
I've just spoken to Pat.

2 I did my homework earlier this morning.
_____

3 I need to tidy my room.
_____

4 Did you clean the car this morning?
_____

5 My friend sent me a really funny video clip about five minutes ago.
_____

6 We went to the museum yesterday.
_____

5 ●●● Choose the correct answers.

Hello from Barbados! I've ¹___ been on a holiday like this before. It's wonderful. We arrived two hours ago but we've ²___ been to the beach and it's amazing. Have you ever ³___ a photo of a Caribbean beach? It's lovely white sand and the sea is a beautiful blue! And I ⁴___ ever felt so hot before – but not uncomfortable. I've ⁵___ swimming and my back ⁶___ already gone brown! I've met some really nice people and we're going to have a meal with them tonight. OK, must stop now because dad has ⁷___ called me. We're going back to the hotel. We haven't unpacked ⁸___!

1	a ever	ⓑ never	c sometimes
2	a yet	b already	c ever
3	a see	b saw	c seen
4	a have	b haven't	c had
5	a been	b go	c was
6	a have	b has	c haven't
7	a already	b yet	c just
8	a ever	b just	c yet

I can identify specific detail in a conversation and talk about outdoor activities.

1 Find eight outdoor activities in the word search. Then label photos A–H below.

V	V	G	I	C	Y	C	L	I	N	G	C
C	L	I	B	Y	P	N	E	N	L	O	F
S	N	O	W	B	O	A	R	D	I	N	G
V	Z	K	C	B	G	S	S	Z	S	N	V
S	H	S	R	K	N	F	Z	T	I	N	C
U	E	Q	L	D	I	J	G	K	N	P	S
R	T	C	F	S	M	Y	I	R	D	Y	K
F	I	Z	H	U	M	H	Z	E	Y	I	I
I	C	I	G	N	I	K	A	D	A	K	I
N	N	U	B	C	W	R	A	G	V	W	N
G	C	J	Z	I	S	V	P	X	E	U	G
K	A	Y	A	K	I	N	G	P	D	A	A

A *fishing*

B _____

C _____

D _____

E _____

F _____

G _____

H _____

2 Complete the sentences with the correct words.

rock   windsurfing   scuba   biking   ~~trekking~~

1 Have you ever been pony *trekking*?
2 We often go mountain _____.
3 I'm going _____ diving in Egypt soon.
4 I'd love to go _____ climbing but it's quite dangerous.
5 I once went _____ but I kept falling into the water!

3 Complete the words from the descriptions.

1 You wear this on your head for protection: h*elmet*
2 You use this to find your way when you are mountain biking: c _____
3 You wear this to keep warm in water: w _____
4 You use these wooden things to move a boat through water: p _____
5 You wear these on your hands for protection: g _____
6 You wear these to protect your eyes: g _____
7 You wear these on your feet when you're climbing: b _____

4 🔊 20 Listen to Adam talking to Emily about his family and the sports they do. Match the people and the sports they do NOW. There are three extra sports.

People
1 [c] Adam
2 [ ] His cousin Ken
3 [ ] His sister
4 [ ] His dad
5 [ ] His brother

Sports
a scuba diving
b swimming
c skiing
d kayaking
e fishing
f mountain climbing
g snowboarding
h windsurfing

I can ask for, give and refuse permission.

1 Choose the correct option.

1 Is *there /it* all right for me to walk through this field?

2 Sure – go *ahead / forward*.

3 *Can / Might* my brother borrow your life jacket?

4 Can I ask *for / a* favour?

5 I'm *frightened / afraid* it's not possible.

6 I'm sorry but you *couldn't / can't* use your phone here.

7 No *problem / worry*. That's fine.

2 Mark sentences from Exercise 1 AFP (asking for permission), GP (giving permission) or RP (refusing permission).

1 *AFP*

2 _____

3 _____

4 _____

5 _____

6 _____

7 _____

3 Order the sentences to make conversations.

1 a ☐ Yes, of course.

  b ☐ Thanks. That's great.

  c ☐ 1 Is it OK for me to use the car later?

2 a ☐ I'm afraid that's not possible. The boat's too small.

  b ☐ Is it all right for my brother to come too?

  c ☐ That's OK. He can stay on the beach.

3 a ☐ I'm sorry but you can't. I'm using them later.

  b ☐ Sure – go ahead.

  c ☐ Can we borrow your skis this morning?

  d ☐ Can I ask you a favour?

4 🔊 21 Match gaps 1–8 with sentences a–h. Then listen and check.

A: Oh, Tom! I like this hotel room. It will be good to share! ¹*h*

B: No problem, Steve. ² ____

A: That's good. And there are two wardrobes. ³ ____

B: Sure – go ahead. ⁴ ____ Mine is a bit small.

A: ⁵ ____ Oh – here's Kerry. Hiya! What's your room like, Kerry?

C: It's cool. Great view! But my wardrobe's really small. ⁶ ____

A: ⁷ ____ We've already filled ours up.

C: That's OK. I'll ask mum and dad.

A: Good idea. Right – I'm going to have a shower before we go to the restaurant.

B: ⁸ ____ I'd like one now too.

C: Sorry Tom – but you can't. I'm in it! Bye …

a Can I have this one?

b Is it all right for me to put some of my dresses in yours?

c I'm afraid that's not possible.

d Yes, of course – there's lots of room.

e I don't mind sleeping by the door.

f Is it all right for me to put my jacket in yours?

g Kerry – is it OK for me to use the shower in your room?

h Is it OK for me to have the bed by the window?

I can write a postcard.

1 Complete the sentences with the correct verbs.

had made ~~bought~~ ate sunbathed went watched visited

1 I've *bought* lots of souvenirs.
2 We _____ on the beach all morning.
3 Mum and dad _____ a museum yesterday.
4 I _____ too much ice cream and I feel sick!
5 Jack and I _____ the sunset. It was beautiful.
6 We _____ a barbecue on the beach on Saturday.
7 I've _____ lots of friends with people my own age.
8 We all _____ to the cinema to see the new James Bond movie.

2 Choose the correct option.

Hi Joe!

¹(Here) / There we are in Bournemouth. We ²'re having / have a great time and the weather has ³had / been brilliant. It's been sunny and hot every day. We're ⁴resting / staying at a top hotel and it's really nice! It's much nicer than camping in a tent. We've been ⁵at / to lots of nice places – and Fran's bought loads of souvenirs! Tomorrow I ⁶'m going / go windsurfing. That's going to be fun! I think I'm going to fall off the board a lot!

⁷See / Seeing you soon!

Lots of love,
Ellie

⁸PS / SP: I've met someone really nice ☺. Tell you all about him next week!

3 Match functions 1–5 with sentences a–e. Then add another sentence for each function from Ellie's postcard.

1 [d] Say where you are: *Here we are in Bournemouth.*

2 [ ] Describe the weather:
_____

3 [ ] Say what you've done:
_____

4 [ ] Talk about your plans:
_____

5 [ ] Ending:
_____

a It's been windy all week.
b Miss you!
c We've had lots of walks.
d I'm writing from my hotel room.
e We're coming home on Monday.

4 Read the email below from your friend Olivia. Write a postcard to Olivia and answer her questions.

a Use the text in Exercise 2 as a model.
b Answer all Olivia's questions.
c Use the Present Perfect to talk about the things you have done so far.
d Use *going to* and the Present Continuous to talk about your plans.

From: Olivia;
To:

I hope you're having a great holiday! Send me a postcard from where you are. Tell me what you've done, what the weather's like and what your plans are. Have you met anyone interesting? I love getting postcards and I collect them!

See you next week,
Olivia

9.8 SELF-ASSESSMENT

For each learning objective, tick (✓) the box that best matches your ability.

😊😊 = I understand and can help a friend.   😦 = I understand but have some questions.

😊 = I understand and can do it by myself.   😦😦 = I do not understand.

		😊😊	😊	😦	😦😦	Need help?	Now try ...
9.1	Vocabulary					Students' Book pp. 106–107 Workbook pp. 102–103	Ex. 1–3, p. 111
9.2	Grammar					Students' Book p. 108 Workbook p. 104	Ex. 4–5, p. 111
9.3	Reading					Students' Book p. 109 Workbook p. 105	
9.4	Grammar					Students' Book p. 110 Workbook p. 106	
9.5	Listening					Students' Book p. 111 Workbook p. 107	
9.6	Speaking					Students' Book p. 112 Workbook p. 108	Ex. 6, p. 111
9.7	Writing					Students' Book p. 113 Workbook p. 109	

9.1   I can talk about landscape, natural features and countries.
9.2   I can use the Present Perfect to talk about experience.
9.3   I can find specific detail in a text and talk about personal adventures.
9.4   I can use the Present Perfect to talk about recent events.
9.5   I can identify specific detail in a conversation and talk about outdoor activities.
9.6   I can ask for, give and refuse permission.
9.7   I can write a postcard.

What can you remember from this unit?

New words I learned (the words you most want to remember from this unit)	**Expressions and phrases I liked** (any expressions or phrases you think sound nice, useful or funny)	**English I heard or read outside class** (e.g. from websites, books, adverts, films, music)

Vocabulary

1 Choose the correct option.

1 On Sunday afternoon we sunbathed on the *coast* / *beach*.
2 We swam across the small *waterfall* / *river* and walked in the *fields* / *rocks*.
3 We went round the *desert* / *island* in a boat.
4 What's the capital *language* / *city* of your country?
5 It's very dangerous to climb up a *volcano* / *jungle*.
6 The *flag* / *border* of my country is blue and white.

2 Complete the sentences with the correct words.

| snowboarding   climbing   diving   fishing
| windsurfing   trekking

1 Young people often go pony _____ in the countryside near my home.
2 My brother fell in the river from the bridge when he went _____ last month.
3 The best place to go scuba _____ is Egypt.
4 I love winter sports. I'm not very good at skiing but I love _____ .
5 We can't go _____ today because there's no wind!
6 My dad goes rock _____ in the mountains every year.

3 Complete the words in the sentences.

1 You should always wear a **l** _ _ _ _ **j** _ _ _ _ _ _ when you're in a boat to keep safe.
2 We went down the river in a **k** _ _ _ _ _ .
3 Oh, no! I lost a **p** _ _ _ _ _ in the water! How are we going to get back to the beach?
4 Don't go cycling without your **h** _ _ _ _ _ _ . It's dangerous. You can hurt your head.
5 I always wear **g** _ _ _ _ _ _ when I'm skiing to protect my eyes from the sun and snow.
6 You can see on the **m** _ _ _ that we're near a forest.

Grammar

4 Complete the sentences with the Present Perfect affirmative form of the verbs.

| buy   drink   forget   leave   see   write

1 I _____ never _____ to do my English homework. It's true!
2 My mum _____ already _____ ten emails this morning! She's still on the computer.
3 Jack and Pete _____ already _____ this film five times. Let's find a different one.
4 My brother _____ already _____ all the milk. I need to get some more from the shop.
5 I'm afraid Helen _____ already _____ the office. You can contact her at home.
6 I _____ never _____ plastic shoes. I think they are uncomfortable.

5 Complete the sentences with the correct form of the Present Perfect.

1 _____ (you/see) the new travel programme yet?
2 We _____ (not have) dinner yet.
3 I _____ (just/speak) to Sally about the hotel arrangements.
4 Tom _____ (already/buy) our train tickets, so don't worry.
5 _____ (your mum/ever/work) in France? Her French is amazing.
6 Lara and Dan _____ (never/be) camping but I think they're going to like it.

Speaking language practice

6 Complete the conversations with one word in each gap.

1 A: _____ I use your goggles, please?
   B: Yes, of _____ you can.
2 A: Is it OK _____ me to leave my bike here?
   B: Sure – _____ ahead.
3 A: Is it all _____ to borrow this wetsuit?
   B: I'm _____ but you can't. I'm going to use it.
4 A: Can we take the boat out today?
   B: I'm _____ that's not a good _____ . The weather's going to get worse.

1 Read definitions 1–8 and find the words in the word search. One word is not in the word search. Which one?

1 fishermen use these to catch fish
2 where the land meets the sea
3 when there aren't many, very unusual
4 protection of the environment
5 a big sea bird
6 a way of doing something
7 this big animal, similar to a tortoise, lives in the sea
8 a part of the sea or land

Missing word: _____

V	C	O	A	S	T	Q	W	E	R
A	T	Y	U	H	B	N	A	O	P
L	A	C	F	G	J	E	H	L	Y
B	R	V	U	K	P	T	O	A	W
A	A	G	K	Y	U	S	I	R	T
T	E	C	H	N	I	Q	U	E	U
R	C	G	T	U	I	O	L	A	R
O	A	W	V	B	T	H	L	U	T
S	E	A	R	A	R	E	U	N	L
S	M	I	G	R	T	W	A	I	E

2 Choose the correct option.

1 Governments need to *order* / *control* fishing so that there are enough fish in the future.
2 Pollution *causes* / *results* many problems in the environment.
3 These birds usually *lie* / *lay* their eggs once a year.
4 If the fishermen *catch* / *take* too many fish, they throw some back into the sea.
5 When I went for a walk along the coast, I *went* / *got* lost.
6 Some baby turtles don't *save* / *survive* the journey to the sea.
7 Big animals *die* / *kill* smaller animals to eat.
8 You can *kill* / *drown* if you don't learn to swim.

3 Choose the correct answers.

1 They had to note everything _____ hand because there were no computers back then.
   A on   B by   C at
2 Nobody knows why the ship disappeared – it's a _____.
   A question   B story   C mystery
3 The fishermen were happy because they had a big _____.
   A catch   B catching   C caught
4 A _____ ship carries scientists and equipment.
   A discover   B research   C results
5 _____ is a big problem in many parts of the world today.
   A Underfishing   B Refishing   C Overfishing
6 Can you tell me the _____ number of words in the essay?
   A perfect   B right   C exact
7 The numbers of cod in the sea are _____.
   A advancing   B increasing   C progressing
8 The scientists _____ how many fish the men have caught.
   A describe   B record   C decide

4 Complete the sentences with words and phrases from Exercises 1, 2 and 3.

1 Birds sometimes get caught in fishing *nets* and drown.
2 I belong to a _____ group and we clean up beaches.
3 Some people steal _____ birds' eggs because they can sell them for a lot of money.
4 The dog is very ill and probably won't _____ until the morning.
5 You must _____ all the results by writing the numbers on this form.
6 I think it's about five o'clock but do you know the _____ time?
7 I love going to the south _____ of Spain where I can swim and sunbathe.
8 I never write my essays _____ – I always type them on my laptop.

5 Make sentences in the correct tense.

1 scientists / try / to learn more about our oceans (Present Continuous)
   Scientists are trying to learn more about our oceans.
2 they / do / this for a long time (Present Perfect)
   _____
3 in 1956, scientists / use / technology to check fish numbers for the first time (Past Simple)
   _____
4 the fishermen / record / how many fish they catch (Present Simple)
   _____
5 this ship / look / for fish (*going to* future)
   _____
6 before this, they / not have / computers (Past Simple)
   _____

6 Read the video script. Underline any words or phrases you don't know and find their meaning in your dictionary.

Can you count fish in the sea?

Part 1

A lot of our planet is a mystery and perhaps the biggest mysteries are our oceans. Scientists are trying to learn about them. One of the most important questions for them is 'How many fish are left in the sea?'

5 Scientists are on a special boat that is leaving from Ullapool in Scotland. They are going to look for fish. But this isn't something new. Scientists have done this for a long time. The ship is the *Scotia* and she's special because she is a research ship. The people who sail on her are studying how many fish there are in Scottish waters. The fishermen throw their

10 nets into the water and catch fish. The scientists look carefully at the results. And this happens every year – the same thing. They have to compare this year's catch with last year's. Is it bigger? Is it smaller? Overfishing is not a new problem. People have been worried about it since the 1950s. Everyone knows that 'fish and chips' is one of the UK's

15 favourite meals. Traditionally the fish is cod. But the number of cod in the North Sea has gone down a lot recently.

The first research ship, the SS *Explorer*, was built in 1956. She was a strong ship with a lot of new machines. For the first time, scientists used technology to check fish numbers. The *Explorer* was the first research

20 ship with a computer! The machine was very big and used special paper. They could put lots of information through this computer. Before this, they had to write everything by hand. It was the beginning of a new and important way of counting fish.

Part 2

25 Today, computers on research ships are faster and cleverer. The scientists put in the numbers of fish and the sizes. But they also put in extra information. They want to find out the age of the fish too. This helps when they plan fishing for the future. Fishermen must not fish in some places.

30 So, how do you know the age of a fish? The scientist takes out a very small bone. It's from the ear. He cuts it in half. There is a circle for every year of the fish's life.

Every fisherman must record how many fish he catches. These fishermen catch fish to sell. It's their job. So they only fish in places where there

35 are lots of fish. The *Scotia* is different. She must also go to places where there were lots of fish in the past but not now. The scientists need to have a better idea of fish populations.

Today, it's good news. Fish numbers are increasing a little in the North Sea. Scientists and fishermen are working together. Perhaps we can't

40 count the exact number of fish in the sea. But we can learn enough to plan and to be sure there is enough fish for us and sea birds in the future.

1 Match sentences 1–6 with notices A–H.

Tip: Read the notices first and try to understand their meanings before you look at the sentences.

1 [D] You can't swim today.
2 ☐ These students have a lesson in a different room.
3 ☐ You can buy something here.
4 ☐ You can get a new pet.
5 ☐ You wear special clothes for this.
6 ☐ Children can't watch this.

A
WANTED
Home for lovely black cat

B
Horror Night 3
18 + only

C
Photography Club
Meetings on Wednesdays and Fridays

D
Pool closed this week

E
END-OF-YEAR PARTY
Everyone in fancy-dress costumes please!

F
Do not feed the animals.

G
Adele's new album!
Now in shop

H
Class 11
Science in Lab 1 not Lab 2 today

2 Read the sentences about a cinema. Choose the best word (A, B or C) for each gap.

Tip: Look at the words that come before and after the gap. Sometimes more than one word gives the right meaning but only one will fit exactly.

1 _____ is a new cinema in our town.
   A It   Ⓑ There   C They
2 It isn't _____ from our house.
   A near   B long   C far
3 The cinema opened _____ 1 May.
   A at   B in   C on
4 The first film there _____ a new horror film.
   A was   B did   C does
5 I'm _____ about horror films.
   A mad   B interested   C passion
6 My brother and I wanted to see the film but it was sold _____.
   A off   B out   C over

3 Complete the conversations.

A See you!

Do you want to go
to the cinema?

B What's on?

C Yes, I am.

Tip: Remember that you are looking for a reply so this must be an answer to a question or a comment about a statement. Sometimes it can be another question asking for details.

1 Do you want to go to the cinema?
  A See you!
  Ⓑ What's on?
  C Yes, I am.
2 How much is the shirt?
  A That's £20.
  B Hold on.
  C Here you are.
3 I've got a good mark in my English test.
  A What a pity!
  B Well done!
  C I don't know.
4 Is the zoo open now?
  A Yes, it was.
  B It's got some lions.
  C I've no idea.
5 I'm going home now.
  A I don't get it.
  B It's not your fault.
  C Catch you later.
6 I'm sorry I'm late.
  A I feel terrible.
  B Is that OK?
  C No problem.

4 Complete the telephone conversation between two friends. Match gaps 1–6 with sentences A–H.

Tip: Look at the sentences before and after the gap to help you choose the correct sentence.

A: Hi, Emma. How are things?
B: ¹*H*
A: I'm a bit tired after the party last night.
B: ² __
A: But it was good! Do you want to go shopping this afternoon?
B: ³ __
A: There's a new sports shop in the High Street. It's very good.
B: ⁴ __
A: I've no idea! I looked in the window but there weren't any prices. We can look.
B: ⁵ __
A: Oh yes. I've got some money. It was my birthday last week. I'm looking for some new boots.
B: ⁶ __
A: Awesome! See you later!

A That's a good idea. I want to buy some new trainers.
B It's my favourite. Do you like it?
C They've got some lovely brown leather ones in Shoe Parade. They're only £30.
D Yes. It finished late!
E I know. It was quite boring.
F Really? Is it expensive?
G Yes, we can. Do you want to buy anything?
H Fine, thanks. And you?

5 Mark the sentences A (right), B (wrong) or C (doesn't say).

Tip: Always read the whole of the text first before looking at the questions. This gives you a general idea about the meaning and helps you find the right places in the text for the answers.

I write to friends in many different countries. It's really interesting to learn about their lives and their cultures and, of course, to go and visit them! I started writing to my English friend, Tina, when I was thirteen. Tina's into sports and music – just like me. We both enjoy swimming but she's fast and I'm not! Also, she listens to a lot of rock music but I hate it. It's very loud!
I stayed with Tina's family last summer in their house in Manchester. They were very kind and they showed me lots of different places in England. I quite liked the cities of Liverpool and Birmingham. But we were in London for three days and that's definitely my favourite city! Of course it's a big and busy city with lots of great shops but it's also got some beautiful parks where you can walk and sit in the sun. I enjoyed walking by the River Thames and looking at the Houses of Parliament and Big Ben, the famous clock.
The weather wasn't very good when I was in England and it rained a lot. But when we were in London it was warm and sunny. It was a fantastic day. I hope Tina can come to France to stay with me this year!

1 Lara writes to a friend in the USA.
   A Right   Ⓑ Wrong   C Doesn't say
2 Lara and Tina have the same interests.
   A Right   B Wrong   C Doesn't say
3 They both enjoy the same type of music.
   A Right   B Wrong   C Doesn't say
4 Tina's family lives in Liverpool.
   A Right   B Wrong   C Doesn't say
5 Lara stayed in London for a weekend.
   A Right   B Wrong   C Doesn't say
6 Tina can speak French well.
   A Right   B Wrong   C Doesn't say

6 Read the article about a safari park. Choose the best word (A, B or C) for each gap.

Tip: Remember that the word you choose has to fit the meaning and the structure of the sentence.

LONGLEAT

We can't all visit other countries to see unusual animals so a ^{1}_____ of people go to zoos. Here the animals stay in cages and can't walk ^{2}_____ fly around. There is another way to see these animals — in safari parks. The ^{3}_____ safari park in England was Longleat which opened ^{4}_____ 1966. Longleat House is the home of ^{5}_____ very rich English family. It's in the south west of England and it ^{6}_____ more than 500 animals. Cars can drive through different parks and you can see ^{7}_____ lions, monkeys, giraffes and tigers. You can ^{8}_____ lovely photographs.

At Longleat there is also a beautiful house to visit and amazing gardens to walk round. Children love ^{9}_____ to Longleat but adults enjoy it too! It's a great day out for everyone in the family.

1 A some   Ⓑ lot   C many
2 A or   B also   C but
3 A one   B beginning   C first
4 A on   B at   C in
5 A a   B an   C the
6 A is   B has   C got
7 A a   B some   C any
8 A take   B make   C do
9 A go   B going   C goes

7 Read the descriptions of some words about entertainment. What is the word for each one? The first letter is already there.

Tip: You might think of a word that starts with the right letter but always check the number of letters to choose the correct word.

1 This is a person who can play an instrument: **m**_usician_

2 If you want to learn about a new film, you can read this: **r** _ _ _ _ _ _

3 This type of film is very funny: **c** _ _ _ _ _ _

4 You can sit in one of these to watch a play or film: **r** _ _

5 This person can get cheap tickets for the cinema because he/she is over sixty-five: **p** _ _ _ _ _ _ _ _ _

6 This is a TV programme about real things, like animals: **d** _ _ _ _ _ _ _ _ _ _ _

8 Complete the comment on a students' website. Write ONE word for each gap.

Tip: Read the whole of the text first, ignoring the gaps, to get an idea of the meaning.

My ¹_name_ is Lily and I'm writing about my beautiful pet. I've ²_____ a lovely dog. She's ³_____ Sunny and she ⁴_____ born in January. She was very small ⁵_____ but now she's six months ⁶_____ and she's big. She eats a ⁷_____ of dog food! She loves ⁸_____ for walks so I take her every day after school. ⁹_____ week I stayed after school for an extra Maths lesson so Sunny ¹⁰_____ go out. She wasn't very happy. Sunny is my pet but she's also my good friend. I ¹¹_____ talk to her about everything!

9 Read the advert and the email. Complete Tom's notes.

Tip: Read the information very carefully. There may be lots of different times, dates etc. in the text – make sure you choose the right one.

Concert in King's Park!
Listen to some great music on Saturday, 10 June.
First band starts at 8.30
Tickets: 16+ £10, under 16 £5
Don't miss it!

From: Alex;
To: Tom;

Do you want to go to the concert? My brother Tim's band is on at 9.00. I've got some free tickets from him! Come round to my house at 8.00 and Tim can take us in his car. Wear something warm and bring some sandwiches. It finishes really late. See you!

Tom's Notes

Concert
Where concert is: ¹_King's Park_
Date: ²_____
Time: ³_____
Where to meet: ⁴_____
Travel to concert by: ⁵_____
Take: ⁶_____

10 Read the email from your English friend, Grace.

Tip: Remember to answer ALL the questions in the email.

From: Grace;
To: Rita;

It's Sara's birthday next week. What can we do to celebrate? We can get a present from you and me – what do you think? What would she like?

Write an email to Grace and answer the questions. Write 25–35 words.

1 Match sentences 1–6 with notices A–H.

Tip: Think about where you might see these signs. It can help you understand their meaning.

1 [B] This place is closed at the weekends.
2 [   ] You mustn't go in the water.
3 [   ] These people can fix a technical problem.
4 [   ] You can't play music here.
5 [   ] Find out about museums and galleries here.
6 [   ] You have to walk carefully.

A
> **Waynes' Room**
> **Stay out!**

B
> **Medical Centre**
> **Open Monday – Friday**

C
> **Got a computer virus?**
> We can help. Call: 07898967895

D
> THIS WAY TO THE
> TOURIST INFORMATION CENTRE →

E
> **Art Exhibition**
> 15 June – 20 August

F
> **Wet Floor!**

G
> **Quiet area**

H
> **No swimming in the river.**

2 Read the sentences about a person and her computer. Choose the best word (A, B or C) for each gap.

Tip: If you don't know the correct word, cross out the ones that you think are wrong.

1 My parents _____ me a new computer for my birthday.
   A paid   B spent   Ⓒ bought
2 It's on the _____ in my bedroom.
   A wardrobe   B sink   C desk
3 I also have a tablet but I need to charge the _____ every day.
   A memory   B battery   C updates
4 I go online in the morning to _____ a social networking site.
   A text   B connect   C use
5 I like going to the cinema so I often check _____ film websites.
   A out   B off   C over
6 Sometimes my _____ hurt because I type on my keyboard for a long time!
   A lips   B fingers   C toes

3 Complete the conversations.

A Yes, you do.

Can I have a
sandwich?

B Help yourself!

C Is it cheese?

Tip: Read the first question or comment very
carefully and imagine an answer before you look
at the choices.

1 Can I have a sandwich?
   A Yes, you do.
   Ⓑ Help yourself!
   C Is it cheese?

2 Do you want to go for a meal?
   A Thanks for the advice.
   B Have some water.
   C Yes, I'm starving!

3 Where should I put my bag?
   A Give me a hand.
   B Why don't you leave it on the floor?
   C You're kidding.

4 How are things?
   A We're all well, thanks.
   B It's not fair.
   C What's the matter?

5 Was the phone expensive?
   A Hold on!
   B That's too bad.
   C It cost a fortune.

6 I feel terrible.
   A That's a terrible idea.
   B You should lie down.
   C You're lucky.

4 Complete the telephone conversation
between two friends. Match gaps 1–6 with
sentences A–I.

Tip: Look for words in the options like 'it' and
'there' that refer back to the sentence before.

A: Do you still live in Green Street?
B: ¹**D**
A: Oh! Is that by the river?
B: ² __
A: We live near there too. Our house is
    opposite the park.
B: ³ __
A: Yes – lots of rooms and a nice garden.
    We're next door to the tourist information
    centre.
B: ⁴ __
A: All through the year really! But it isn't too
    noisy. Why don't you come round one
    evening?
B: ⁵ __
A: That's a good idea. And after that we can
    walk along the river.
B: ⁶ __
A: Cool! See you then.

A Great. How about this Wednesday?
B I like that house a lot.
C Is it usually very busy in the summer?
D No, we moved last month. Now we live in
   Bank Road.
E I can't come this week.
F I know those houses. They're lovely.
G I got some interesting information there.
H I'd love to. We can do some homework
   together.
I Yes, I can see it from my bedroom. It's very
   pretty.

5 Read Chrissy's blog. Mark the sentences A (right), B (wrong) or C (doesn't say).

Tip: Sometimes you need to read more than one sentence to find the correct answer to a question.

I was born fifteen years ago in a village in the countryside. It's very small with just a few shops, a post office and a church. We had to travel for half an hour by car to do our shopping at a supermarket every week! I went to a village school and there were only sixty children in the whole school. I knew everyone and it was like a big family. Then two years ago my dad changed jobs and we moved to a really big town. I was very excited about it because I found life in the country quite boring! I couldn't buy fashionable clothes there and there wasn't a cinema or a night club! We sometimes went swimming at the leisure centre but there was nothing else to do.

Now, I would really like to go back to the countryside! Life in a big town is fun and we often go to museums, theatres and other interesting places but I miss the peace and quiet! There are always cars in our street, even at night and it's so busy in the shops. You have to wait for a long time to pay for things. My school is very, very big. There are hundreds and hundreds of students and I don't know all the teachers. When I leave school I want to go back and live in a quieter place!

1 Chrissy's first home was in a village.
   Ⓐ Right   B Wrong   C Doesn't say

2 There wasn't a supermarket in the village.
   A Right   B Wrong   C Doesn't say

3 Chrissy lived in the countryside until she was fifteen.
   A Right   B Wrong   C Doesn't say

4 Her family moved to a town so Chrissy could go to a bigger school.
   A Right   B Wrong   C Doesn't say

5 Chrissy didn't enjoy the free time activities she could do in the village.
   A Right   B Wrong   C Doesn't say

6 Chrissy prefers living in the countryside to living in the town.
   A Right   B Wrong   C Doesn't say

6 Read the article about the first computer. Choose the best word (A, B or C) for each gap.

Tip: Read the whole text first, ignoring the gaps, to get an idea of the general meaning.

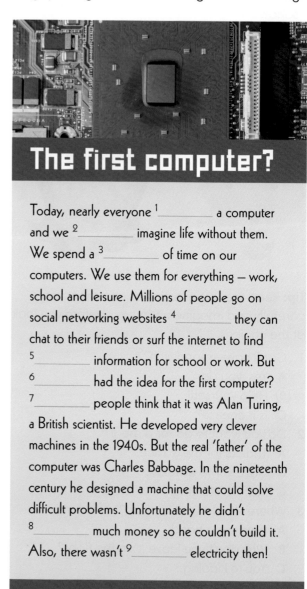

The first computer?

Today, nearly everyone ¹_____ a computer and we ²_____ imagine life without them. We spend a ³_____ of time on our computers. We use them for everything – work, school and leisure. Millions of people go on social networking websites ⁴_____ they can chat to their friends or surf the internet to find ⁵_____ information for school or work. But ⁶_____ had the idea for the first computer? ⁷_____ people think that it was Alan Turing, a British scientist. He developed very clever machines in the 1940s. But the real 'father' of the computer was Charles Babbage. In the nineteenth century he designed a machine that could solve difficult problems. Unfortunately he didn't ⁸_____ much money so he couldn't build it. Also, there wasn't ⁹_____ electricity then!

1 A having   B got   Ⓒ has
2 A didn't   B aren't   C can't
3 A much   B lot   C some
4 A where   B which   C that
5 A on   B out   C of
6 A who   B which   C why
7 A Much   B Lot   C Many
8 A had   B have   C has
9 A some   B any   C an

7 Read the descriptions of some words about the body and health. What is the word for each one? The first letter is already there.

Tip: Check if you need a singular or plural word.

1 You use this part of the body to think with: **b**_rain_

2 When you eat, your food goes here:
   s _ _ _ _ _ _ _

3 You make this to see a doctor at a certain time:
   a _ _ _ _ _ _ _ _ _ _ _

4 You go here when you are very ill:
   h _ _ _ _ _ _ _

5 If you are ill, you must tell the doctor about these:
   s _ _ _ _ _ _ _ _

6 Your dentist checks these:
   t _ _ _ _

8 Complete the email. Write ONE word for each gap.

Tip: Decide if you need to find a verb, a noun, an adjective, an article or something else.

To: terry@hello.com

Hi Terry,
How ¹**are** you? ²_____ you see the doctor this morning? I hope you're
³_____ better now. I think I've
⁴_____ a cold too! Or perhaps it's
hay ⁵_____. I sneeze every time I go into the garden. Last year my doctor gave me ⁶_____ tablets but I don't always remember ⁷_____ take them! Yesterday I went to the gym. Martin ⁸_____ go because I think he's ill too. I did ⁹_____ much exercise and I hurt my shoulder. I ¹⁰_____ to rest it at the moment. This is NOT a good week!
Anyway, it's time to finish. I ¹¹_____ do some homework!
Love,
Amanda

9 Read the advert and the email. Complete Phil's notes.

Tip: Remember to copy the correct spelling of any names in the information.

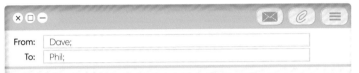

Ron's Repairs!
Has your computer got a virus?
Has your computer crashed?
I can fix it!
Bring your computer to me at 11, Africa Drive
OR
Phone me and I can come to your house
07345213785
Cheap rates for students!

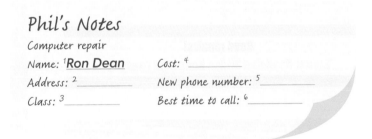

From: Dave;
To: Phil;

Have you still got a problem with your computer? Here's an advert that could help! I know Ron Dean – he's very good. He lives near you in Africa Drive, number 11. He only charges £6 an hour for students. He's got a new phone number: 07643842198. It's best to call him in the evening. Or see him at school. He's in Class 12B. Good luck!

Phil's Notes
Computer repair
Name: ¹**Ron Dean**   Cost: ⁴_____
Address: ²_____   New phone number: ⁵_____
Class: ³_____   Best time to call: ⁶_____

10 Read the email from your friend, Mike.

Tip: Remember to use the right beginning and ending for your email.

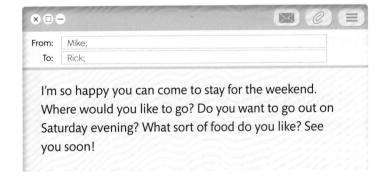

From: Mike;
To: Rick;

I'm so happy you can come to stay for the weekend. Where would you like to go? Do you want to go out on Saturday evening? What sort of food do you like? See you soon!

Write an email to Mike and answer the questions. Write 25–35 words.

1 Match sentences 1–6 with notices A–H.

Tip: Don't worry about the words you don't know. You should still understand the notices.

1 [A] Go here for cheap food.
2 [ ] You can try on new clothes here.
3 [ ] Students have to be quiet here.
4 [ ] You don't need to bring your own equipment.
5 [ ] People have to use the stairs.
6 [ ] You cannot walk here today.

A
Level 3
Zorro's – 50% off all meals

B
Coastal path closed
until Friday

C
Apologies
Escalators not working at the moment

D
Road repairs!
Tanner Road and Bridge Road next Tuesday

E
No speaking in exam room

F
School concert tickets
On sale in school office from Monday

G
Changing rooms at back of the shop

H
Beach Hire Shop Surfboards – £5 per hour.

2 Read the sentences about a shopping centre. Choose the best word (A, B or C) for each gap.

Tip: Think about the meaning AND the grammar of the word you need.

1 A new shopping centre _____ in our town last month.
   A began   (B) opened   C built

2 It's quite _____ our school.
   A close   B near   C next

3 There are some very _____ clothes shops.
   A enjoyable   B interested   C trendy

4 My brother has a _____ as a waiter in one of the cafés there.
   A job   B work   C place

5 My friend and I _____ shopping there yesterday.
   A got   B made   C went

6 Unfortunately I lost my _____ in the department store.
   A wallet   B sales   C price

3 Complete the conversations.

Tip: Sometimes an option may be right for the situation but not exactly the right reply for the question.

A The changing rooms are over there.

Can I help you? B Have you got any winter coats?

C What's up?

1 Can I help you?
   A The changing rooms are over there.
   (B) Have you got any winter coats?
   C What's up?
2 Would you like to come to my party?
   A It's going to be a surprise.
   B Give me a break!
   C When is it?
3 I bought the last concert ticket.
   A What a nightmare!
   B Well done!
   C That's not a good idea.
4 Is it OK for us to wait here?
   A Please wait for me.
   B I don't think this will happen.
   C I'm sorry but you can't.
5 I've lost my phone.
   A Thanks for telling me.
   B Sure – go ahead.
   C When did you last use it?
6 I've got a computer problem.
   A Fingers crossed.
   B Can I help?
   C I get the message.

4 Complete the telephone conversation between two friends. Match gaps 1–6 with sentences A–I.

Tip: Remember to read the whole conversation after you've chosen the answers to check that it makes sense.

A: Hi! You look very relaxed.

B: ¹*I*

A: Lucky you! Where did you go?

B: ²__

A: That's a beautiful area. Was the weather good?

B: ³__

A: I went swimming at the beach last week and it was really cold. I only stayed in for five minutes. But that was on the east coast. I've never been to Bournemouth.

B: ⁴__

A: What a great idea! Thanks, I'd love to. I'll try and save some money.

B: ⁵__

A: Great! I got a new tent for my birthday. I haven't used it yet.

B: ⁶__

A: Yes, it is. No problem. Next year you'll be nice and dry.

A We go camping. It won't be very expensive.

B Well, it rained for the first three days but then we had some sun. The sea was very warm.

C Dad drove us there and it took five hours.

D We went to the south coast, near Bournemouth.

E I must show you some photographs later.

F Cool! Is it big enough for two people? My tent is old and the rain gets in.

G We want to go back there again next year because it was a lot of fun. Would you like to come with us?

H Don't worry. You can stay in my tent.

I I've just been on holiday for two weeks!

5 Read part of an article about people's summer jobs. Mark the sentences A (right), B (wrong) or C (doesn't say).

Tip: The questions come in the same order as the information in the text.

I'm Jade. I'm eighteen and I've just finished secondary school. I'm going to university in September to study Maths. A few months ago I decided to look for a summer job because I'll need some money when I'm at university! I looked online and I found an excellent job as a tour guide in my city. But it's an unusual tour guide job!

Usually a tour guide takes tourists to popular sights in a city and tells them about the history of the different places. I do that but I don't do it during the day. I do it at night! Every Monday and Thursday evening I take a small group of tourists to old buildings in the city. It's a 'ghost' tour and I tell them about the people who lived and died in the houses. I also tell them ghost stories about the places. We go in the dark without any lights and it's a bit scary! But the tourists love it and I love it too! It's much more interesting than working in a supermarket.

1 Jade is studying at secondary school.
  A Right   Ⓑ Wrong   C Doesn't say
2 Jade wanted a job for a short time.
  A Right   B Wrong   C Doesn't say
3 Jade found her job in a magazine.
  A Right   B Wrong   C Doesn't say
4 Jade has worked as a tour guide before.
  A Right   B Wrong   C Doesn't say
5 Jade's job is full-time.
  A Right   B Wrong   C Doesn't say
6 Her job can be quite frightening.
  A Right   B Wrong   C Doesn't say
7 Jade thinks the job is better than being a shop assistant.
  A Right   B Wrong   C Doesn't say
8 The tourists give Jade extra money because she's a good tour guide.
  A Right   B Wrong   C Doesn't say

6 Read the article about a famous department store. Choose the best word (A, B or C) for each gap.

Tip: Read the whole of the sentence with the gap and try to guess what the missing word might be.

Harrods

Harrod's is one of the ¹_____ famous department stores in the world. A ²_____ of celebrities (and even the Queen of England) ³_____ bought things there. Harrod's is in Knightsbridge which is an expensive area ⁴_____ London. ⁵_____ are seven floors and 330 different departments! Harrod's employs more ⁶_____ 4,000 people and fifteen million customers visit the store every year. You ⁷_____ buy nearly everything there, from T–shirts to houses! In the 1970s people could buy unusual pets. They even sold lions! The store is very big today but ⁸_____ it started in 1849 it only had one room. Then it ⁹_____ sell very much — only tea and groceries. In 1883 there was a bad fire in Harrod's but then they built it bigger and better than before. In 1898 it was one of the first places in the world that had an escalator.

1 A more   Ⓑ most   C best
2 A many   B some   C lot
3 A have   B did   C are
4 A on   B at   C in
5 A They   B There   C It
6 A that   B than   C of
7 A must   B have   C can
8 A time   B what   C when
9 A didn't   B hasn't   C wasn't

7 Read the descriptions of some words about work and school. What is the word for each one? The first letter is already there.

Tip: Check if you're looking for a person, place, thing or an adjective.

1   This is a person who paints pictures: a*rtist*

2   This is a person who writes stories for newspapers: **j** _ _ _ _ _ _ _ _ _

3   If you want to borrow books, you go here: **l** _ _ _ _ _ _ _

4   Students look at this to find out where their lessons are:
t _ _ _ _ _ _ _ _

5   A person is this if they don't have a job: **u** _ _ _ _ _ _ _ _ _

6   This is a person who is in the same class as you: **c** _ _ _ _ _ _ _ _ _

8 Complete the email. Write ONE word for each gap.

Tip: Sometimes you need to read the sentence after the gapped sentence to find the right word.

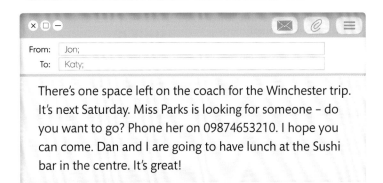

To: mia@hello.com

Hi Jack,
I hope you ¹*are* well. I need some advice! The teacher ² _ _ _ _ _ _ just given us our English test results. My results were ³ _ _ _ _ _ _ very good! They're worse ⁴ _ _ _ _ _ _ last term. I'll have to take another test ⁵ _ _ _ _ _ week. Please tell me – What ⁶ _ _ _ _ _ _ I need to revise? Is it OK if I ask you ⁷ _ _ _ _ _ _ questions about grammar in my next email? I really ⁸ _ _ _ _ _ _ understand some of the tenses. ⁹ _ _ _ _ _ _ you finished your term tests yet? I ¹⁰ _ _ _ _ _ _ stand this time of year! Outside ¹¹ _ _ _ _ _ _ sun is shining and I want to go to the beach. But I have to stay inside and study for tests!
Write soon,
Mia

9 Read the advert and the email. Complete Katy's notes.

Tip: You won't need all the information in the notice or email. Read the notes carefully to choose the right information.

> ## School trip to Winchester
>
> For all students in Year 10.
> We leave at 8.15 from school and get back at 5.30.
> Morning – visit to castle. Lunch – your choice.
> Afternoon – cathedral and shopping!
>
> ## Only £15
> ## Sign list below by Friday.

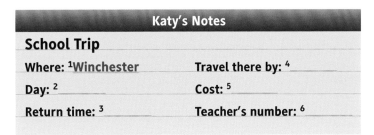

From: Jon;
To: Katy;

There's one space left on the coach for the Winchester trip. It's next Saturday. Miss Parks is looking for someone – do you want to go? Phone her on 09874653210. I hope you can come. Dan and I are going to have lunch at the Sushi bar in the centre. It's great!

Katy's Notes	
School Trip	
Where: ¹**Winchester**	**Travel there by:** ⁴ _ _ _ _
Day: ² _ _ _ _	**Cost:** ⁵ _ _ _ _
Return time: ³ _ _ _ _	**Teacher's number:** ⁶ _ _ _ _

10 Read the email from your English friend, Harry.

Tip: Make a quick plan for your email and note down what to include.

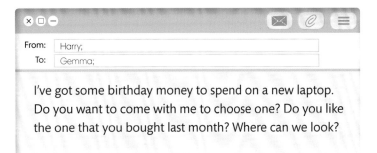

From: Harry;
To: Gemma;

I've got some birthday money to spend on a new laptop. Do you want to come with me to choose one? Do you like the one that you bought last month? Where can we look?

Write an email to Harry and answer the questions. Write 25–35 words.

Unit 1

Exercise 1
1 drums 2 classical 3 actor 4 romantic
5 cartoons 6 salsa

Exercise 2
1 playing 2 listening 3 taking 4 reading
5 watching 6 drawing

Exercise 3
1 Where do you live?
2 Does your dad work every day?
3 How many English lessons do you have a week?
4 Do you go swimming every Saturday?
5 How often does your friend take photos?
6 What music do your sisters like?

Exercise 4
1 f 2 e 3 c 4 b 5 a 6 d

Exercise 5
1 Do 2 don't 3 does 4 Does 5 doesn't 6 do

Exercise 6
1 I don't like documentaries.
2 Do you want to go to the cinema?
3 My friend doesn't live near me.
4 Jack speaks English and French.
5 Our teacher usually gives us lots of homework.
6 What time do you go to bed on Fridays?

Exercise 7
1 on 2 Can 3 screening 4 sold
5 seat 6 much

Unit 2

Exercise 1
1 pyjamas 2 trainers 3 tattoo
4 baggy 5 belt 6 scarf

Exercise 2
1 untidy 2 interesting 3 cheerful
4 frightening 5 worried 6 irritating

Exercise 3
1 is wearing 2 is Mike going
3 'm not doing / 'm doing
4 Is Dan driving / is 5 isn't working /
's sleeping 6 are you phoning

Exercise 4
1 are you doing 2 're reading 3 read
4 'm sitting 5 'm trying 6 don't want
7 always wear 8 wear 9 Do you want

Exercise 5
1 in 2 at 3 on 4 at 5 on 6 in

Exercise 6
1 a 2 b 3 a 4 a 5 b

Unit 3

Exercise 1
1 snake 2 bear 3 monkey 4 duck
5 rabbit 6 claw

Exercise 2
1 aggressive 2 shy 3 forgetful 4 impulsive
5 adventurous 6 careless

Exercise 3
1 protect 2 brush 3 empty 4 give
5 scratch 6 take

Exercise 4
1 I was in bed early last night.
2 Were your parents at the concert on Saturday?
3 That programme wasn't very interesting.
4 Was Tom at your party?
5 What was your favourite film last year?
6 There weren't any monkeys at the safari park.

Exercise 5
1 was / didn't like 2 did you live / moved
3 didn't work / was 4 Did you watch / didn't / were
5 phoned / didn't answer / Were you
6 Did the teacher explain / was

Exercise 6
1 so / all / totally 2 feel / No / happen
3 accident / could 4 can't / forgive

Unit 4

Exercise 1
1 console 2 battery 3 pen drive 4 keyboard
5 digital camera 6 tablet

Exercise 2
1 check 2 chat 3 text 4 charge 5 make
6 click

Exercise 3
1 connect 2 crashed 3 died 4 stopped
5 download 6 virus

Exercise 4
1 forgot 2 left 3 didn't give
4 Did the computer cost 5 took 6 stole

Exercise 5
1 watching 2 working 3 to go 4 helping
5 to learn 6 to feed

Exercise 6
1 who 2 where 3 which 4 where
5 which 6 who

Exercise 7
1 ago 2 all 3 At 4 after 5 later 6 end

Unit 5

Exercise 1
1 b 2 c 3 c 4 a 5 c 6 a

Exercise 2
1 make 2 sweep 3 do 4 empty
5 tidies 6 took

Exercise 3
1 gallery 2 station 3 centre 4 hall
5 office 6 Information Centre

Exercise 4
1 hard 2 angrily 3 well 4 carefully
5 quickly 6 early

Exercise 5
1 don't have to 2 can 3 mustn't
4 can't 5 has to/must 6 mustn't

Exercise 6
1 Can you give me some advice?
2 Where do you think we should go?
3 I think you should go to the British Museum.
4 I don't think that's a good idea.
5 Why don't you go to an art gallery?
6 Thanks for the advice.
7 That's a great idea.

Unit 6

Exercise 1
1 stomach 2 skin 3 beard 4 ankle
5 muscles 6 teeth

Exercise 2
1 c 2 a 3 b 4 c 5 b 6 b

Exercise 3
1 temperature 2 allergy 3 hay
4 headache 5 throat 6 flu

Exercise 4
1 much 2 many 3 any 4 lot
5 isn't 6 some

Exercise 5
1 Where were you going when I saw you this morning?
2 Hannah was reading a book when Gary called at her house.
3 I wasn't working when Dave came to visit us.
4 Were you waiting at the bus stop when it started to rain?
5 The teacher shouted at us because we weren't concentrating in class today.
6 Were you having dinner when I phoned you earlier?

Exercise 6
1 matter / got / should 2 feeling / hurts / appointment
3 wrong / feel / down / some

Unit 7

Exercise 1
1 bunch / florist's 2 loaf / bakery 3 bag / greengrocer's
4 bottle / pharmacy 5 bar / newsagent's
6 pair / shoe shop

Exercise 2
1 escalator 2 trolley 3 court 4 department
5 toilets 6 shopper

Exercise 3
1 pocket 2 change 3 much 4 sales 5 piggy
6 wallet/purse

Exercise 4
1 more interesting 2 bigger 3 the most enjoyable
4 as comfortable 5 cheaper

Exercise 5
1 How much money are you going to spend on Saturday?
2 My dad is going to look for a new job soon.
3 I'm playing tennis with Erica at 2.30 today.
4 When are you arriving back from holiday?
5 I'm going to try to do my homework this evening.

Exercise 6
1 d 2 e 3 b 4 c 5 a

Unit 8

Exercise 1
1 journalist 2 mechanic 3 accountant
4 electrician 5 architect 6 lawyer

Exercise 2
1 for 2 in 3 as 4 at 5 earn 6 were
7 in 8 for

Exercise 3
1 pupils 2 staff 3 head 4 playground
5 library 6 classmates

Exercise 4
1 won't be / 'll watch 2 Will you stay 3 won't get / 'll go
4 will be / 'll be able 5 Will you be / 'll phone 6 won't finish

Exercise 5
1 Will / fails 2 go / will be 3 will move / gets
4 will you / close 5 don't / won't be

Exercise 6
1 We will definitely be late.
2 I probably won't see you later.
3 They might arrive soon.
4 Will you definitely come to the party?
5 She might not want a big meal.
6 It may rain later.

Unit 9

Exercise 1
1 beach 2 river / fields 3 island 4 city 5 volcano
6 flag

Exercise 2
1 trekking 2 fishing 3 diving 4 boarding 5 surfing
6 climbing

Exercise 3
1 life jacket 2 kayak 3 paddle 4 helmet 5 goggles
6 map

Exercise 4
1 have never forgotten 2 has already written
3 have already seen 4 has already drunk
5 has already left 6 have never bought

Exercise 5
1 Have you seen 2 haven't had 3 've just spoken
4 has already bought 5 Has your mum ever worked
6 have never been

Exercise 6
1 Can / course 2 for / go 3 right / sorry 4 afraid / idea